Why the Government is failing… "We the People"
Published by Craft Creek Publishing
Copyright 2020 John M. Zito
ISBN: 9798678859259

Cover by Vila Design

Why the Government is failing…
"We the People"

John M. Zito

Contents

Preamble – I Love my Country 1

Chapter 1 – Where it all began...5

Chapter 2 – Foreign Affairs (a history lesson)..................................9

Chapter 3 – Infrastructure 24

Chapter 4 – Healthcare...49

Chapter 5 – Education...65

Chapter 6 - Gun Control..72

Chapter 7 – Economics 107

Chapter 8 – Environmental 119

Chapter 9 – COVID-19 127

Final Word 145

Charities 149

Bibliography..152

Acknowledgments...161

About the Author 163

PREAMBLE – I LOVE MY COUNTRY

"The world is a book, and those who do not travel, read only a page"
- Saint Augustine

Question:

Why do you think America is the greatest country in the world?

Answer:

"It's not the greatest country in the world. That is my answer. There is absolutely no evidence to support the statement that we're the greatest country in the world. We're 7th in literacy, 27th in math, 22nd in science, 49th in life expectancy, 178th in infant mortality, 3rd in median household income, number 4 in labor force, and number 4 in exports. We lead the world in only three categories, number of incarcerated citizens per capita, number of adults who believe angels are real, and defense spending (where we spend more than the next 26 countries combined, 25 of whom are our allies). So, when you ask what makes America the greatest country in the world, I don't know what the f#@k you are talking about. We sure used to be. We stood up for what was right. We fought for moral reasons. We passed laws, struck down laws for moral reasons. We waged wars on poverty, not poor people. We sacrificed. We cared about our neighbors. We put our money where our mouths were, and we never beat our chests. We built great big things, made ungodly technological advances, explored the universe, cured diseases, and we cultivated the world's greatest artists and the world's greatest economy. We reached for the stars… We aspired to intelligence. We didn't belittle it. It didn't make us feel inferior. We didn't identify ourselves by who we voted for in the last election and we didn't scare so easy. We were able to be all these things and do all these things

because we were informed, by great men, men who were revered. The first step in solving any problem is recognizing there is one. America is not the greatest country in the world anymore." From the TV show, The Newsroom, A college student asks a panel "can you say why America is the greatest country in the world"? This was Will McAvoy's, response. [1]

If those words and numbers surprised you, you're not alone. They should be shocking. Our country should be doing better. My goal is to demonstrate why America is not the greatest country in the world anymore, and why we can point to our government for blame. I will make suggestions on how we can improve on the categories just mentioned: literacy, math, science, life expectancy, infant mortality, exports, etc., so we can start to regain the status that is expected of us.

I love my country and what it stands for... Life, Liberty, and the Pursuit of Happiness. I am not an expert on any of the topics that I present in this book. I am not an economist. I am not a radical nor a conspiracist. I don't have extreme political views. I am not a civil engineer. I am no expert on foreign policy, nor do I pretend to be an expert on education, healthcare, or environmental matters.

I am an average American, who grew up in an apartment in Queens, New York in a lower-middle-class environment. I don't have strong ties to either political party and consider myself a moderate. I am registered as a Republican but have voted for Democrats. I lean towards candidates that share my views and how to improve our standard of living. As an American, I am tired and fed up with America falling far behind in almost every measurable category.

Our Founding Fathers created our government and thus the United States of America. In our very short history, we were the first to fly an airplane, we invented electricity, the light bulb, the automobile, the cell phone, the personal computer, Wi-Fi, and the internet. For God's sake, we put a man on the moon!

We are a resilient country. We have overcome a Civil War, two World Wars, disasters (both manmade and natural), the Great Depression, the Great Recession, and 9/11. We are a great country, but there is tremendous room for improvement, and we have much to learn from other nations.

I have been fortunate enough that, over the past 30 years, my job has allowed me to travel all over the world. Between business and personal travel, I have visited:

AFRICA
Morocco: Casablanca, Rabat, Tangier

ASIA
India: Agra, Bangalore, Mumbai, New Delhi, Pune
Singapore

AUSTRALIA
Sydney

EUROPE
Austria: Linz, Melk, Salzburg, Vienna
Belgium: Brussels
England: London, Manchester
France: Cannes, Normandy, Paris
Germany: Munich, Passau
Hungary: Budapest
Italy: Rome, South Tyrol
Portugal: Lisbon
Slovakia: Bratislava
Spain: Cadiz, Malaga, Marbella

NORTH AMERICA
Bahamas: Nassau
Bermuda
British and US Virgin Islands
Canada: Quebec City, Toronto
Dominican Republic: Punta Cana
Mexico: Mexico City, Playa Del Carmen
Puerto Rico: San Juan

SOUTH AMERICA
Chile: Santiago
Aruba

I have traveled extensively to many of these locations. In the early 1990s, as part of a global system rollout, twice I spent six weeks traveling around the world. Those trips started out in New Jersey, then to Los Angeles, then two weeks in Sydney, a week in Singapore, two weeks in Brussels, a week in London, and then back home. My company was acquired by a German company in the mid-1990s, and since then I have visited Germany over 100 times. For two years, I spent one week a month in Germany. I have traveled to Toronto about 30 times and London about 20 times. I have traveled to India 4 times. From 2015-2017 I commuted from New Jersey to Hartford, Connecticut every other week (firsthand experience with our rail systems).

This book details my observations during these travels and what I have learned during my time abroad. It is about what I believe that we, the United States of America, can do better, regarding the economy, healthcare, education, the environment, and basic infrastructure. For each chapter of this book, I will point out where I feel this country, or our government, is deficient, and I will provide examples of where other nations and their administrations are doing a better job. Some of these examples will shock you. This book is not about making America great again. It is about improving our quality of life, not having children go to bed hungry, providing a safe learning environment so children are not afraid to go to school, having a Congress, regardless of their party affiliation, that wants to work side-by-side on improving and advancing our country. It's about… *We the People of the United States, in Order to form a more perfect Union, establish Justice, insure domestic Tranquility, provide for the common defense, promote the general Welfare, and secure the Blessings of Liberty to ourselves and our Posterity.*" [2] Together (united), we can make a difference!

I will be donating 100 percent of the net proceeds of this book to charity. I will highlight some of the charities throughout the book. A full list of charities can be found in the appendix.

CHAPTER 1 – WHERE IT ALL BEGAN

"Let us not be unmindful that liberty is power; that the nation blessed with the largest portion of liberty must in proportion to its numbers be the most powerful nation upon earth."
- John Quincy Adams

First, let us recap where we, as a country, stand today. (Hint: it's not great.) Our financial system is fragile, due to COVID-19 and the shutdown of our economy. On March 9, 2020, the Dow dropped 2000 points, the largest single-day loss in the history of the stock exchange. (Chapter 9 COVID-19).

Our national debt sits at a staggering **$23.25 trillion** and is growing at an alarming rate. It is the largest deficit in our history. (Chapter 7 Economics).

We are still haunted by one of the deadliest school shootings in United States history, where 17 people were killed at Marjory Stoneman Douglas High School in Florida on February 14, 2018. Four months earlier, on October 1, 2017, Stephan Paddock killed 58 people and injured over 500 when he opened fire from a Las Vegas hotel overlooking a concert attended by 22,000 people, making this the deadliest mass shooting ever. (Chapter 6 Gun Control).

Our infrastructure is crumbling. Since 2014 there have been 26 Amtrak derailments. Our road surfaces are a disaster. Bridges and tunnels built in the 1930s are collapsing or crumbling around and under us, and need to be replaced. Based on a report released by TRIP titled <u>National Bridge News Release</u>, as of 2012, *"a total of 25 percent of the nation's bridges (20 feet or longer) are either structurally deficient or functionally obsolete. Eleven percent of America's bridges are structurally deficient, meaning there is significant deterioration of the bridge deck, supports or other major components. Bridges that are structurally deficient may be posted for lower weight limits or closed if their condition warrants such action. An additional 14 percent of the nation's bridges are functionally obsolete. Functionally obsolete bridges no longer meet current highway design standards, often due to narrow lanes, inadequate clearances or poor alignment with the approaching roadway"* [3] (Chapter 3 Infrastructure).

Our students are significantly outpaced by other countries, particularly in math. (Chapter 5 Education).

We find ourselves with troops deployed in Afghanistan and Iraq. We are at odds with Iran and North Korea regarding nuclear weapons. The Russians have just been indicted for using social media to tamper with the 2016 presidential election. (Chapter 2 Foreign Affairs).

Our healthcare system is a laughingstock. Between what was introduced by President Obama and then recently overhauled by President Trump, no one really knows what it takes to get it right while not hurting those that need it the most. Compared to 10 of our peer countries in healthcare statistics, we rank dead last. We have the highest infant mortality rate compared to those same countries. Yes, that shocked me too. (Chapter 4 Healthcare).

We are running out of natural resources at a catastrophic rate, and we are experiencing more frequent and severe natural catastrophes due to global warming. The 2017 Atlantic hurricane season will long be remembered as one of the busiest and most destructive seasons on record. (Chapter 8 Environmental).

If we compare where we are as a country today, to any other point in our history, there are some similarities to the late 1920s, especially regarding the Stock Market crash and the eventual Great Depression. Looking at this period, we will see how the government played a vital role in turning the country around. (Chapter 3 Infrastructure).

During my travels and as I made these observations, the question I kept asking myself was, how did we get here? How did things get this bad? When did the government start failing us? My conclusion is that we actually experienced a perfect storm between two major factors. So, when, exactly, did the government start failing us? Let's take a closer look.

The first factor coincided with the Gilded Age. "The Gilded Age is a period in American society (between the Civil War and World War I) with rapid economic growth but also characterized by corruption, materialism, monopolistic businesses, and growing inequality.

The Gilded Age was a time of unbridled capitalism, with some business leaders becoming very wealthy through the consolidation of key industries into powerful monopolies.

The term 'Gilded Age' implies that the outer wealth was a mask for inner corruption and inner poverty. 'Gilded Age' is a satire on the rich monopolists, who were accused of gaining wealth through monopolistic practices, mistreatment of workers, and corruption of the political process". [4]

Greed! It became the driving factor, and for the first time in the history of the United States, we had some very wealthy and powerful men who would drive the government and their agendas, including how we handled foreign affairs and what was in the best interest of big business. Coincidentally, this is also the same time that we started to see intense lobbying occurring. Technically, the First Amendment allows for lobbying. It states: *"Congress shall make no law respecting an establishment of religion, or prohibiting the free exercise thereof; or abridging the freedom of speech, or of the press; or the right of the people peaceably to assemble, and to petition the Government for a redress of grievances"* [5] The last statement, *"petition the Government for a redress of grievances"*, technically allows for lobbying, but up until this point, lobbying was "practiced discreetly". [6]

The second factor in why our government is failing us has to do with the **national divide**. This divide results from our two-party system, and the fact that the chasm is growing wider and wider. The divide can also be seen between the upper vs. lower class, conservatives vs. liberals, and, some would argue, blacks vs. whites. What we end up with is people and political parties at the extreme ends of the spectrum. We have become a polarized nation. I could probably write an entire book on how we became a polarized nation and suggestions on how to fix it, but instead, I'll leave that to the experts. Here are three books on the topic:

1. <u>Why We're Polarized</u>, by Ezra Klein
2. <u>The Big Sort</u> by Bill Bishop
3. <u>The Great Alignment: Race, Party Transformation, and the Rise of Donald Trump</u>, by Alan I. Abramowitz

An article written by Nicole Sinclair titled <u>Harvard Professor Identifies the "Worst Nightmare" in America right now</u>, highlights the findings of a Harvard Business School study on US Competitiveness led by Professors Michael Porter, Jan Rivkin, and Mihir Desai.

"We've concluded after these five years of work on this that actually the political system and the political rhetoric is the problem at the core," Porter said. "Because of the political gridlock we've not been able to make any progress on a lot of the basics." The political system is hindering economic development in America.

"I'm an economist and the last thing I thought I would end up doing when I got into this project was to actually start deeply studying the political system," Porter told Yahoo Finance. "But we've now concluded that's where the root cause of where America is today. We have a lot of strengths. We are very dynamic. We have tremendous people. We have a lot of assets. We're just stalled."

"Today, we believe that our political system is now the major obstacle to progress on the economy, especially at the federal level," according to the report.

Sinclair writes "Meanwhile, trust for political leaders has declined significantly over the George W. Bush and Barack Obama administrations, according to the report. In 1958, three out of four Americans trusted their government. Today less than one in five trust their governments to do the right thing." [7]

It's now up to us, as Americans, to force change! Remember the wise words of Abraham Lincoln at his Gettysburg address: *"A government of the people, by the people, for the people, shall not perish from the Earth."*

CHAPTER 2 – FOREIGN AFFAIRS (A HISTORY LESSON)

"Earth provides enough to satisfy every man's needs, but not every man's greed."
\- **Mahatma Gandhi**

I don't have to tell you that, throughout American history, there have been many great achievements especially as it relates to expansion. We can look back to the goals of Manifest Destiny and the exploration of Lewis and Clark and the Louisiana Purchase as examples. Equally, there have been times when the United States abused its strength and interfered with other governments for the sole purpose of greed. There are also countless occasions where the United States has sided with or aided other countries or terrorist organizations for our political gain, without considering long-term implications of these actions.

Philippines

Ferdinand Magellan, the Portuguese explorer sailing for Spain, claimed the Philippines in the name of Spain in 1521. By 1565, much of the archipelago came under Spanish rule. In 1898, the Unites States defeated Spain in the Spanish-American War, and the Philippines became a US territory.

Much debate occurred at the Senate level as to how to handle the occupation of the Philippines. Unfortunately, for the Filipino people and the ensuing rebellion, US retaliation resulted in a bloodbath.

As part of these debates and according to Oliver Stone and Peter Kuznick, authors of <u>The Untold History of the United States</u>, *Senator Richard Pettigrew called the betrayal of Filipino independence "the greatest international crime of the century." Filipino citizens overwhelmingly supported the rebels and provided them food and shelter. The Americans, some of whom employed the tactics they had perfected while fighting Native Americans, responded with extraordinary brutality. Following one ambush,*

General Lloyd Wheaton ordered all towns within a twelve-mile radius to be destroyed and all their inhabitants killed. When rebels surprised the Americans stationed at Balangiga on the island of Samar, killing fifty-four of the seventy-four men there, Colonel Jacob Smith ordered his troops to kill everyone over the age of ten and turn the island into "a howling wilderness." Some of the soldiers happily obliged. [8]

[Senator Albert] Berveridge was a huge supporter of the US occupation and was pushing for a permanent government to be established. Beveridge was the only senator to visit the Philippines firsthand. In January of 1900, Beveridge addressed the Senate chamber.

"MR. PRESIDENT, I address the Senate at this time because senators and members of the House on both sides have asked that I give to Congress and the country my observations in the Philippines and the Far East, and the conclusions which those observations compel; and because of hurtful resolutions introduced [condemning the American occupation] and utterances made in the Senate, every word of which will cost and is costing the lives of American soldiers.

Mr. President, the times call for candor. The Philippines are ours forever, "territory belonging to the United States," as the Constitution calls them. And just beyond the Philippines are China's illimitable markets.

This island empire is the last land left in all the oceans. If it should prove a mistake to abandon it, the blunder once made would be irretrievable.

...But to hold it will be no mistake...The Philippines give us a base at the door of all the East. Lines of navigation from our ports to the Orient and Australia, from the Isthmian Canal to Asia, from all Oriental ports to Australia converge at and separate from the Philippines. They are a self-supporting, dividend-paying fleet, permanently anchored at a spot selected by the strategy of Providence, commanding the Pacific. And the Pacific is the ocean of the commerce of the future. Most future wars will be conflicts for commerce. The power that rules the Pacific, therefore, is the power that rules the world. And, with the Philippines, that power is and will forever be the American Republic.

...Mr. President, self-government and internal development have been the dominant notes of our first century; administration and the

development of other lands will be the dominant notes of our second century.
...

...The Constitution declares that "Congress shall have power to dispose of and make all needful rules and regulations respecting the territory belonging to the United States." Not the Northwest Territory only; not Louisiana or Florida only; not territory on this continent only but any territory anywhere belonging to the nation.

...[The] power to administer government anywhere and in any manner would have been in Congress if the Constitution had been silent; not merely because it is a power not reserved to the States or people; not merely because it is a power inherent in and an attribute of nationality; not even because it might be inferred from other specific provision of the Constitution; but because it is the power most necessary for the ruling provisions of our race--the tendency to explore, expand, and grow, to sail new seas and seek new lands, subdue the wilderness, revitalize decaying peoples, and plant civilized and civilizing governments all over the globe.

...Do you tell me that it will cost us money? When did Americans ever measure duty by financial standards? Do you tell me of the tremendous toil required to overcome the vast difficulties of our task?

...Mr. President and Senators, adopt the resolution offered that peace may quickly come and that we may begin our saving, regenerating, and uplifting work. Adopt it, and this bloodshed will cease when these deluded children of our islands learn that this is the final word of the representatives of the American people in Congress assembled. Reject it, and the world, history and the American people will know where to forever fix the awful responsibility for the consequences that will surely follow such failure to do our manifest duty.

How dare we delay when our soldiers' blood is flowing?" [8]

The US occupation of the Philippines and the ensuing Philippine-American War resulted in a staggering number of lives lost. The occupation had horrific similarities to the genocide of the Native Americans. *"In the fifteen years that followed the defeat of the Spanish in Manila Bay in 1898, more Filipinos were killed by US forces than by the Spanish in 300 years of colonization."* [9]

The motive? Expand trade to Asia-Pacific.

Latin America

When it comes to our neighbors to the south, the US has a history of intervening with the internal affairs of countries throughout Latin America. The primary reasons for US intervention? To promote our own interests and to cater to US "big business" exploitation.

Cuba

Similar to the Philippines, in 1898, as a result of the Spanish-American War, Spain ceded Cuba to the US.

Companies like Bethlehem Steel and the United Fruit Company quickly staked claim to Cuban land and resources. It is estimated that by 1901, US businesses owned over 80 percent of Cuban minerals. [8]

In 1902, Cuba was granted independence from the United States. Cuba's first president, Tomas Estrada Palma, worked with the US to put in place the Cuban constitution, which included the Platt Amendment, basically giving the US the right to intervene whenever it deemed necessary and securing the Guantánamo naval base.

Over the next few years, the US supported Cuban politicians who provided US investors with business and banking opportunities.

From 1906-1909, the US occupied Cuba after Palma resigned due to a rebellion led by Jose Miguel Gomez.

In 1933, Gerardo Machado was overthrown in a coup led by Sergeant Fulgencio Batista. Batista was very supportive of American interests and increased business relations by agreeing to allow casinos, modeled after Las Vegas, to be built in Cuba. The following year, in 1934, the US gave up its right to intervene in Cuba's internal affairs, although this was much truer on paper than in practice.

Let's fast forward to 1956, when Fidel Castro, with the support of Ernesto "Che" Guevara, waged a guerrilla war. The US, sensing Batista's defeat, withdrew military aid to his cause. The following year, Castro led his guerilla troops into Havana, forcing Batista out.

In 1960, all US businesses in Cuba were nationalized without compensation. In response, the US broke off diplomatic relations with Havana and imposed a trade embargo.

In March of that year, President Eisenhower approved a plan for the CIA to train Cuban exiles with the intent of invading Cuba and overthrowing Castro. The CIA used Guantánamo Bay to train a small army in assault landings and guerilla warfare. When President John F. Kennedy was elected in November 1960, he was briefed on the plan. In February of 1961, President Kennedy authorized the attack but wanted to disguise any US involvement, so the landing spot of the invasion was changed to a swampy area known as the Bay of Pigs. Furthermore, eight US World War II bombers were painted to look like Cuban aircraft. The plan was for two airstrikes, originating from Nicaragua, to bomb Cuban airfields. The first airstrike on April 15th missed most of its targets. When President Kennedy learned of the news, he ordered the second airstrike to be canceled. Basically, all of Castro's air force was intact when the exiles landed in Cuba on April 17th. There wasn't much of a fight. Twelve hundred exiles surrendered and over 100 were killed. This event came to be known as the "Bay of Pigs fiasco". At that point, Castro declared Cuba a communist state and started an alliance with the USSR. That same year, the CIA drew up at least five different plans to assassinate Castro, known as Operation Mongoose.

1962 brought us the Cuban missile crisis when Castro allowed the USSR to deploy nuclear missiles on the island. That triggered a crisis between the US and USSR, which, if not for President Kennedy and Soviet leader Nakita Khrushchev sorting things out personally, would have resulted in a nuclear war.

To this day, relations between the US and Cuba remain strained. For a brief period, President Obama, hoping to improve diplomatic ties, allowed Americans to travel to Cuba. That was shut down again when President Trump took office.

The Panama Canal

Looking to establish a shipping route connecting the Atlantic and Pacific oceans, the US set its sights on the Isthmus of Panama. The only problem - Panama was a province of Colombia at that time. In November 1903, the US and Panama signed the Hay–Bunau-Varilla Treaty, giving the US exclusive rights to build a canal for the price of $10 million dollars. However, the treaty was never ratified by Colombia's Senate. This would not stop President Teddy Roosevelt; the US convinced the Panamanian Nationalists to declare their independence from Columbia. The US offered naval support by sending the warship USS Nashville to impede any interference from Colombia.

The Panama Canal was inaugurated on August 15, 1914. It wasn't until December 1999, after decades of protest and negotiations, that the US passed control of the canal over to Panama.

Chile

In 1973, the CIA, through covert operations, took part in the military coup to overthrow Salvador Allende, of Chile's democratically elected Popular Unity government. In 1998, 25 years later, some of the documents were declassified. Based on an article <u>Chile and the United States: Declassified Documents Relating to the Military Coup</u> published by Peter Kornbluh, those documents included the following:

- *Cables written by US Ambassador Edward Korry after Allende's election, detailing conversations with President Eduardo Frei on how to block the president-elect from being inaugurated. The cables contain detailed descriptions and opinions on the various political forces in Chile, including the Chilean military, the Christian Democrat Party, and the US business community.* [10]
- *CIA memoranda and reports on "Project FUBELT"--the codename for covert operations to promote a military coup and undermine Allende's government. The documents, including minutes of meetings between Henry Kissinger and CIA officials, CIA cables to its Santiago station, and summaries of covert action in 1970, provide a clear paper trail to the decisions and operations against Allende's government* [10]

- *National Security Council strategy papers which record efforts to "destabilize" Chile economically, and isolate Allende's government diplomatically, between 1970 and 1973.* [10]
- *State Department and NSC memoranda and cables after the coup, providing evidence of human rights atrocities under the new military regime led by General Pinochet.* [10]
- *FBI documents on Operation Condor--the state-sponsored terrorism of the Chilean secret police, DINA. The documents, including summaries of prison letters written by DINA agent Michael Townley, provide evidence on the car bombing assassination of Orlando Letelier and Ronni Moffitt in Washington D.C., and the murder of Chilean General Carlos Prats and his wife in Buenos Aires, among other operations.* [10]

Argentina

At the same time, Henry Kissinger was backing the military coup in Chile in 1973, he is accused of giving Argentina approval for a "dirty war", which ended up killing 30,000 people. This is based on declassified US state department documents. Duncan Campbell published the article <u>Kissinger approved Argentinian 'dirty war'</u> in December 2003.

Henry Kissinger gave his approval to the "dirty war" in Argentina in the 1970s in which up to 30,000 people were killed, according to newly declassified US state department documents.

Mr. Kissinger, who was America's Secretary of State, is shown to have urged the Argentinian military regime to act before the US Congress resumed session, and told it that Washington would not cause it "unnecessary difficulties".

The revelations are likely to further damage Mr. Kissinger's reputation. He has already been implicated in war crimes committed during his term in office, notably in connection with the 1973 Chilean coup.

The material, obtained by the Washington-based National Security Archive under the Freedom of Information Act, consists of two memorandums of conversations that took place in October 1976 with the visiting Argentinian foreign minister, Admiral César Augusto Guzzetti. At the time, the US Congress, concerned about allegations of widespread human rights abuses, was poised to approve sanctions against the military regime.

According to a verbatim transcript of a meeting on October 7, 1976, Mr. Kissinger reassured the foreign minister that he had US backing in whatever he did.

The revelations, which were also announced at a conference in Argentina [in December 2003]*, confirm suspicions at the time that the regime would not have continued to carry out atrocities unless it had the tacit approval of the US, on which it was dependent for financial and military aid...* [11]

The Rest of the Region

Stone and Kuznick point out that in the early 20th century, *"defending American businessmen's growing investments required the constant involvement of the military to prop up corrupt and dictatorial governments and suppress revolutionary movements. As early as 1905, [Secretary of War Elihu] Root, who had become secretary of state, wrote candidly, 'The South Americans now hate us, largely because they think we despise them and try to bully them.' Between 1900 and 1925, the United States repeatedly intervened militarily in Latin America. It sent troops to Honduras in 1903, 1907, 1911, 1912, 1919, 1924, and 1925; to Cuba in 1906, 1912, and 1917; to Nicaragua in 1907, 1910, and 1912; to the Dominican Republic in 1903, 1914, and 1916; to Haiti in 1914; to Panama in 1908, 1912, 1918, 1921, and 1925; to Mexico in 1914; and to Guatemala in 1920. The only reason the United States didn't intervene more frequently was that it often stayed, occupying countries for extended periods of time: Nicaragua from 1912 to 1933, Haiti from 1914 to 1933, the Dominican Republic from 1916 to 1924, Cuba from 1917 to 1922, and Panama from 1918 to 1920."* [8]

The Middle East

Like most Americas, I believe there is no place on this earth for terrorists and I will never forgive the cowards responsible for the 9/11 attacks that killed 2,977 of our fellow citizens. In my opinion, our government was partly at fault based on some shockingly poor decisions made across the Middle East. Did you know that it was the United States that assisted Iran with establishing its nuclear capabilities, or that we backed Iraq and Saddam Hussein during the Iran-Iraq War, or worse yet, that we armed and trained Osama bin Laden during the Soviet-Afghan War? Does that give anyone else a knot in their stomach? Over the decades, the United States has repeatedly destabilized the region.

Let's take a brief look at the history of US involvement in the Middle East.

Iran

Starting in 1908, the British government had control over Iran's oil reserves through the Anglo-Iranian Oil Company (which would later be renamed British Petroleum - BP).

Mohammad Mossadegh was elected Prime Minister in 1951 on his promise to gain back control of Iran's natural resources. This concerned both the UK and the US for two reasons: 1) losing control over the oil and 2) a threat that Iran could fall behind the Iron Curtain.

In 1953, the CIA and the British Intelligence agency MI6 staged a military coup to overthrow Mossadegh. Documents admitting CIA involvement were released on the 60th anniversary of the coup and published on the National Security Archive as part of the Freedom of Information Act.

The US supported Iran's monarch, Mohammad Reza Pahlavi, to rule as Shah of Iran. Iranians resented the foreign interference, fueling anti-American sentiment in the country for decades to come. [12]

In 1957, the US and Iran signed a civil nuclear cooperation agreement under which the US provided technology and resources that eventually led to Iran's controversial nuclear program. [12]

In 1979, a revolution in Iran caused the Shah to flee and eventually wind up in the United States to receive treatment for his cancer. The Iranians once again saw the US as meddling, and wanted the Shah returned. Ayatollah Khomeini became the supreme leader of the Islamic Republic. [12]

Later that year, Iranian students stormed the US embassy in Tehran and took 52 American hostages. This was directly related to President

Jimmy Carter's decision to allow the Shah into the United States. *"The students demand the Shah be extradited to Iran to stand trial for 'crimes against the Iranian people.' After 444 days, Iran releases the hostages in exchange for state assets being unfrozen -- minutes after President Ronald Reagan is sworn into office. During the crisis, the US cuts all diplomatic ties with Iran. Formal diplomatic relations have never been restored. The Shah died in July 1980."* [12]

In 1980, war broke out between Iran and Iraq. The bad blood between the US and Iran only got worse after the US decided to back Iraq and Saddam Hussein. Those not old enough to remember 40 years ago might find this hard to believe, but it was very real. The US provided several billion dollars' worth of economic aid, the sale of dual-use technology, non-US origin weaponry, military intelligence, and special operations training. [13]

The following details the embarrassing fiasco known as the Iran-Contra Affair (you cannot make this shit up!):

"The Iran–Contra affair was a political scandal in the United States that occurred during the second term of the Reagan Administration. Senior administration officials secretly facilitated the sale of arms to Iran, which was the subject of an arms embargo. They hoped, thereby, to fund the Contras in Nicaragua while at the same time negotiating the release of several US hostages. Under the Boland Amendment, further funding of the Contras by the government had been prohibited by Congress.

The scandal began as an operation to free seven American hostages being held in Lebanon by Hezbollah, a paramilitary group with Iranian ties connected to the Army of the Guardians of the Islamic Revolution. It was planned that Israel would ship weapons to Iran, and then the United States would resupply Israel and receive the Israeli payment. The Iranian recipients promised to do everything in their power to achieve the release of the hostages. Large modifications to the plan were devised by Lieutenant Colonel Oliver North of the National Security Council in late 1985, in which a portion of the proceeds from the weapon sales was diverted to fund anti-Sandinista, or Contras, in Nicaragua.

Under the Shah of Iran, the United States was the largest seller of arms to Iran, and the vast majority of the weapons that the Islamic Republic of Iran inherited in January 1979 were American. To maintain this arsenal,

Iran required a steady supply of spare parts to replace those broken and worn out. After Iranian students had stormed the American embassy in Tehran in November 1979 and taken 52 Americans hostage, President Jimmy Carter had imposed an arms embargo on Iran. After Iraq invaded Iran in September 1980, Iran had a desperate need for weapons and spare parts to maintain its current weapons. After Ronald Reagan took office as President on 20 January 1981, he vowed to continue Carter's policy of blocking arms sales to Iran under the grounds that Iran was a supporter of terrorism. A group of senior Reagan administration officials in the Senior Interdepartmental Group conducted a secret study on 21 July 1981, which concluded that the arms embargo was ineffective as Iran could always buy arms and spare parts for its American weapons elsewhere while at the same time, the arms embargo opened the door for Iran to fall into the Soviet sphere of influence as the Kremlin could sell Iran weapons if the United States would not. The conclusion was that the United States should start selling Iran arms as soon as it was politically possible to keep Iran from falling into the Soviet sphere of influence. At the same time, the openly declared goal of Ayatollah Khomeini to export his Islamic revolution all over the Middle East and overthrow the governments of Iraq, Kuwait, Saudi Arabia and the other Persian Gulf states led to the Americans perceiving Khomeini as a major threat to the United States. In the spring of 1983, the United States launched Operation Staunch, a wide-ranging diplomatic effort to persuade other nations all over the world not to sell arms or spare parts for weapons to Iran. The reason why the Iran–Contra affair proved so humiliating for the United States was that American diplomats, as part of Operation Staunch had-been lecturing other nations about how morally wrong it was to sell arms to the Islamic Republic of Iran and applying strong pressure to prevent any arms sales to Iran." [14]

Bin Laden

Once again, the US made a poor choice in supporting and funding the Islamic radicals fighting the Russians in Afghanistan. One of these extremists, Osama Bin Laden, was the son of a wealthy Saudi Arabian businessman. (Okay, perhaps "poor choice" is an understatement…)

Journalist Robert Dreyfuss writes: *In the decades before 9/11, hard-core activists and organizations among Muslim fundamentalists on the far right were often viewed as allies for two reasons, because they were seen as fierce anti-communists and because they opposed secular nationalists such as Egypt's Gamal Abdel Nasser and Iran's Mohammed Mossadegh.*

By the end of the 1950s, rather than allying itself with the secular forces of progress in the Middle East and the Arab world, the United States found itself in league with Saudi Arabia's Islamist legions. Choosing Saudi Arabia over Nasser's Egypt was probably the single biggest mistake the United States has ever made in the Middle East.

A second big mistake occurred in the 1970s, when, at the height of the Cold War and the struggle for control of the Middle East, the United States either supported or acquiesced in the rapid growth of the Islamic right in countries from Egypt to Afghanistan.

Still another major mistake was the fantasy that Islam would penetrate the USSR and unravel the Soviet Union in Asia. It led to America's support for the jihadists in Afghanistan. America's alliance with the Afghan Islamists long predated the Soviet invasion of Afghanistan in 1979 and had its roots in CIA activity in Afghanistan in the 1960s and in the early and mid-1970s (some speculate that the US involvement in Afghanistan is what led the Soviets to invade). The Afghan jihad spawned civil war in Afghanistan in the late 1980s, with funding to militants, known as the mujahideen, which eventually giving rise to the Taliban, and got Osama bin Laden started on building Al Qaeda.

Would the Islamic right have existed without US support? Of course. But there is no question that the virulence of the movement that we now confront—and which confronts many of the countries in the region from Algeria to India and beyond—would have been significantly less had the United States made other choices during the Cold War. [15]

The Washington Post reported in 2002: *"The United States spent millions of dollars to supply Afghan schoolchildren with textbooks filled with violent images and militant Islamic teachings ….*

The primers, which were filled with talk of jihad and featured drawings of guns, bullets, soldiers and mines, have served since then as the Afghan school system's core curriculum. Even the Taliban used the American-produced books …." [15]

Based on an article posted on WashingtonsBlog: *Bin Laden was a product of a monumental miscalculation by western security agencies. Throughout the 80s he was armed by the CIA and funded by the Saudis to wage jihad against the Russian occupation of Afghanistan.*

After Ronald Reagan was elected in 1981, US funding of the mujahideen increased significantly and CIA Paramilitary Officers played a big role in training, arming and sometimes even leading mujahideen forces.

The CIA trained the mujahideen in many of the tactics Al Qaeda is known for today, such as car bombs, assassinations and other acts that would be considered terrorism today. [15]

Iraq

In an article entitled <u>US Secretly Gave Aid to Iraq Early in Its War Against Iran</u> written by Seymour M. Hersh in 1992, he reports *"The Reagan Administration secretly decided to provide highly classified intelligence to Iraq in the spring of 1982 -- more than two years earlier than previously disclosed -- while also permitting the sale of American-made arms to Baghdad in a successful effort to help President Saddam Hussein avert imminent defeat in the war with Iran, former intelligence and State Department officials say.*

The American decision to lend crucial help to Baghdad so early in the 1980-88 Iran-Iraq war came after American intelligence agencies warned that Iraq was on the verge of being overrun by Iran, whose army was bolstered the year before by covert shipments of American-made weapons.

The New York Times and others reported last year that the Reagan Administration secretly decided shortly after taking office in January 1981 to allow Israel to ship several billion dollars' worth of American arms and spare parts to Iran. That intervention and the decision to aid Iraq directly in 1982 provide evidence that Washington played a much greater role than was previously known in affecting the course of the long and costly Iran-Iraq War.

The interventions also raise questions about the White House's often-stated insistence in the early 1980's that it was remaining neutral in the

Iran-Iraq War, since the United States was arming both sides in its desire to see neither side dominate the vital oil region.

In the end, officials acknowledged, American arms, technology and intelligence helped Iraq avert defeat and eventually grow, with much help from the Soviet Union later, into the regional power that invaded Kuwait in August 1990, sparking the Persian Gulf War." [17]

"America must learn from the foreign policy mistakes of our past. These mistakes have led to the creation of our enemies, such as Saddam Hussein, Manuel Noriega, and Osama Bin Laden.

The enemy of our enemy is not always our friend, most often they become our enemies too." [15]

As you can see, the US has not always made the best choice – or with the right motivation – when it comes to dealings with foreign relations. Many of the decisions are directly related to the situations we find ourselves in today.

Charity - Heart 911

"HEART 9/11 (Healing Emergency Aid Response Team 9/11) is a team of first responders - FDNY, NYPD, PAPD and the NYC Building Trades - that bonded in the aftermath of September 11, 2001 to honor the sacrifices of brave colleagues and family members lost, to continue to utilize their experience and training in service to others and to bring a message of hope to communities affected by disaster. HEART 9/11's mission is to Respond immediately to natural and man-made disasters; Rebuild community centers in hard-hit areas to meet grass roots needs; Recover by building resiliency for individuals, families and communities."

Website heart911.org

CHAPTER 3 – INFRASTRUCTURE

We shape our buildings; thereafter they shape us.
- Winston Churchill

You and I come by road or rail, but economists travel on infrastructure.
- Margaret Thatcher

What is infrastructure, exactly? When you hear the word, what comes to mind? Roads? Bridges? Train tracks? It's all of that and more. Our infrastructure is the basic physical and organizational foundation our civilization is built on. Our infrastructure affects how we move around in our world, how and where we live, and how we communicate. It's vitally important. And ours is decaying.

As part of my job, I frequently travel between Princeton, New Jersey, and Hartford, Connecticut, along part of what is known as the Northeast Corridor. Comprising major cities such as Boston, New York, Philadelphia, Baltimore, and Washington, D.C., this stretch is home to about 52 million people and makes up about 20 percent of our GDP. By 2050, the population is estimated to grow to over 70 million. And yet, the transportation system is painfully inadequate.

To drive between Central New Jersey and Hartford without traffic (I'll pause here for laughs) takes about 3.5 hours. Traffic being unavoidable, I typically choose to take the train. If you've never been on one of these trains, I can't accurately convey to you just how antiquated the service is. Fun fact: I actually found the inspiration to write this book during a 20-minute stop in New Haven, Connecticut to change the engine from electric to diesel. How in the world is this happening in this corridor of this country?

The US has a decided lack of high-speed rail, and I got to wondering why that is. I should be able to get from Central New Jersey to Hartford in less than half the time it currently takes. Let's do a real-life comparison. The distance from Trenton, New Jersey to Hartford, Connecticut is 181 miles. It takes about 4 hours to travel by direct train service between these locations.

That averages out to about 45 miles per hour. I'll compare that to a trip I took with my family in 2015, from London to Paris, which is about 283 miles. The direct train service from London to Paris took 2 hours and 16 minutes. That averages out to roughly 125 miles per hour. The distance is over 100 miles longer and yet it took about half the time as the Trenton to Hartford trip. So what's the problem? If you guessed our government, you're correct.

The biggest barrier to improved rail service in the United States is simply the lack of political will. At the federal level, support for passenger rail service has languished, and Washington has delegated decision-making (and increasingly, funding) to the states. Even states like Texas that have tried to implement bullet trains connecting the larger cities have faced voter opposition, which could be due simply to a lack of public education about the benefits. Some of the obvious pros, of course, are fewer cars on the road, which is not only greener, but also leads to fewer accidents, and a boon for the economy.

Let's take a look at how the United States compares to other countries when it comes to investing in rail infrastructure.

China leads the way in national rail investment, followed by Switzerland, Austria, India, and the UK. The US comes in 13th, just ahead of Turkey. [18] We are way too tied to our cars, folks.

It wasn't always this way of course. The US once prided itself on its railroads and people looked forward to train travel. However, by the mid-20th Century, the government's focus shifted to highways and air travel, and railroads were all but forgotten. Public transportation ceased to be a priority.

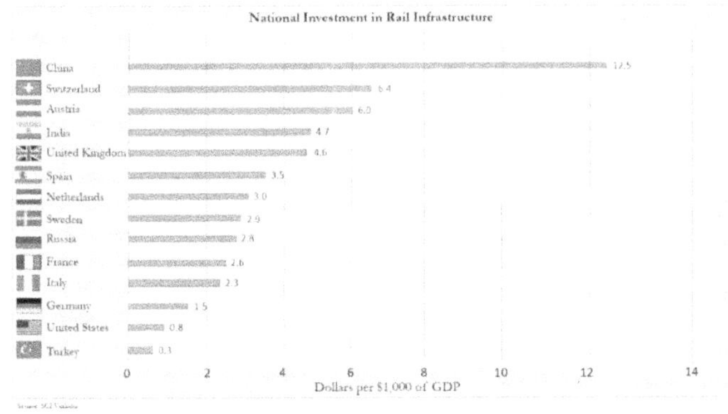

Quality of Railroad Infrastructure

1 - Extremely Underdeveloped 7 - Extensive and Efficient

Rank	Country	Value
1	Switzerland	6.8
2	Japan	6.6
3	Hong Kong	6.4
4	France	6.3
5	Singapore	5.7
6	Finland	5.7
7	Germany	5.7
8	Spain	5.7
9	Netherlands	5.7
10	Korea	5.6
11	Tawain	5.5
12	Austria	5.3
13	Belgium	5.2
14	Luxembourg	5.2
15	Canada	5.0
16	United Kingdom	5.0
17	Malaysia	4.9
18	**United States**	**4.8**
19	Denmark	4.8
20	Lithuania	4.7
21	Sweden	4.7
22	China	4.6
23	Czech Republic	4.6
24	Ukraine	4.5
25	Slovak Republic	4.5
26	Portugal	4.5
27	India	4.4
28	Australia	4.3
29	Kazakhstan	4.3
30	Russia	4.2

Source: World Economic Forum, Executive Opinion Survey

What Can We Learn from European Trains?

Author Jon Worth put forth several areas in which the US could learn and adopt from European rail systems after the deadly Amtrak derailment in Philadelphia several years ago, and I want to explore some of those here.

Speed was the major factor in the Philly derailment, a highly unlikely occurrence in Europe due to Automatic Train Protection, which restricts speed and automatically hits the brakes if limits are exceeded. Of course, this relies on proper installation. The train in Philly was equipped with this precaution but the track was not, and at the risk of making Europe sound above reproach, two derailments have occurred there due to a failure to install the protection.

We need more federal investment in safer rail, not less. This one shocked me - immediately following the Philly train accident, the House voted to reduce federal funding for Amtrak. I don't know about you, but I can't quite wrap my head around that one. We're a nation already far too reliant on personal automobiles. If train fares increase due to decreased federal funding, we'll be even more tied to our cars which, despite the rail safety issues outlined here, are still generally less safe than trains.

The US needs better oversight and accountability when it comes to our rails. No fewer than eight different companies own our tracks and rail systems. This makes it even more difficult for an already disinterested federal government to even know where to invest what money it does allocate. This is not good.

Lastly, we Americans need to remember that, although safety measures must be increased, train travel is still safer than car travel. You are more likely to die on your drive to the train station than you are on the train. Getting that word out would go a long way toward getting us out of our cars and into a safer mode of travel - and perhaps increased funding due to increased passenger demand. [19]

The Politics of the New York Subways

Having grown up riding the New York City Subway system and having ridden on various subway systems around the world, I can tell you that the NYC subway system is an embarrassment. I can also tell you that, by far, the best subway system I have ridden is in Singapore.

In June of 2017, New York Governor Andrew Cuomo declared that the city of New York's subway system was in a state of emergency. An investigation by the New York Times revealed that leaders ignored and therefore allowed the problem to exacerbate for years.

The New York subways are old, crumbling, and fraught with problems, and yet, the transit authority's budget has barely changed (when adjusted for inflation) in a quarter-century. In that time, daily use has doubled. Stories of breakdowns, delays, fires, power outages, and overcrowded cars are so commonplace as to almost be boring. New York is actually the only major city in the world that has seen a decline in track miles since World War II. How does that happen? In our biggest city?

The Times also found that, regardless of party, leaders have repeatedly failed the city's subways by either cutting budgets or simply redirecting that money to their own interests. Add in that many public officials take contributions from transit authority unions and contractors, and you have projects with bloated budgets and inefficient planning.

An entire separate book could be written about the problems occurring beneath the city of New York, but the point I want to drive home is the direct connection between the crumbling subway and the government. Repeated failures to maintain, update, and expand fall squarely on the shoulders of those whose job it is to run and protect the city. It's a microcosm of what's happening all over the country, and something needs to change. [20]

Bridges & Roads

According to Trip.org, a national transportation research non-profit organization, one-quarter of America's more than 600,000 bridges are deficient and in need of repair or replacement. That's 150,000 bridges, folks. An additional 14 percent are functionally obsolete, meaning they don't meet current design standards. And that was citing data from the Federal Highway Administration's National Bridge Inventory in 2012. Eight years later, I think it's safe to assume things haven't miraculously improved.

We've all seen the horrific news stories about bridge collapses. Don't think it can't happen to you, where you live. These stats are extremely concerning.

Pennsylvania comes in as the state with the most deficient bridges at 24 percent, followed closely by Oklahoma at 23 percent. Iowa, Rhode Island, and South Dakota round out the states that come in at greater than 20 percent deficient. If you're feeling a little bridge-phobic right about now, you might consider a move to Washington, Utah, Arizona, Texas, Nevada, or Florida, which all rank at 5 percent or less in bridge deficiency.

Bridges are costly and complicated to construct. Fixing existing structures creates even more complexities as drivers must find alternate routes and face delays. But it must be done, and our leaders must step up. [21]

Of course, it's not just the bridges that are in poor condition. Data from TRIP, a National Transportation Research group, show that nearly 30 percent of roads in the US are in such poor condition that resurfacing isn't an option. They need to be ripped up and rebuilt. And these potholes, ruts, and cracks aren't simply a nuisance - they hit drivers squarely in the wallet. It's estimated that bad roads cost drivers an average of $515 a year in extra car maintenance costs.

As with the bridges, where you live makes a difference. Ironically, the worst roads are in Washington, DC, with 92 percent of the roads in poor condition, and none rated in good condition. I suppose we can at least be glad our federal officials aren't simply spending all the money on their own roads. California tops the list of states with bad roads at 51 percent, followed by Rhode Island at 45 percent, New Jersey at 40 percent, and Michigan and Washington at 39 percent. The states with the best road conditions? Florida, Missouri, Nevada, Minnesota and Arkansas all come in at 10 percent or less.

If you live in one of the worst states, that $515 figure quoted above balloons to as much as $1,042 in DC, or add an extra $762 in maintenance costs in California.

The solution here is simple if unpopular: increase road funding by raising the federal gas tax. It's estimated that the average driver pays less than $100 per year in federal gas taxes, a number that hasn't changed since the early 90s. This shortfall has resulted in a game of catch-up, where we're scrambling to fix bad roads instead of maintaining and building high-quality roads. [22]

Quality of Roads

1 - Extremely Underdeveloped 7 - Extensive and Efficient

Rank	Country	Value
1	France	6.5
2	United Arab Emirates	6.5
3	Singapore	6.5
4	Portugal	6.4
5	Oman	6.4
6	Switzerland	6.4
7	Austria	6.3
8	Hong Kong	6.3
9	Finland	6.1
10	Germany	6.1
11	Netherlands	6.0
12	Saudia Arabia	6.0
13	Spain	5.9
14	Japan	5.9
15	Luxembourg	5.9
16	Canada	5.9
17	Korea	5.8
18	Bharain	5.8
19	Denmark	5.7
20	**United States**	**5.7**
21	Tawain	5.7
22	Cyprus	5.6
23	Chile	5.6
24	United Kingdom	5.6
25	Sweden	5.6
26	Belgium	5.5
27	Malaysia	5.4
28	Ireland	5.4
29	Croatia	5.3
30	Iceland	5.2

Source: World Economic Forum, Executive Opinion Survey

What's Going on in the Rest of the World?

Before we dive into what's going on around the globe, let's look at where the US falls into a few other categories. According to a report from the World Economic Forum (WEF), it's not all bad news here. Our infrastructure still ranks in the top 11 globally. The US comes in fifth in the quality of air transport structure. We come in 15th in railroad infrastructure and 14th in road quality. Interestingly, we're 99th for mobile phone subscriptions. The Forum found that several countries, including the US and Germany, have seen deteriorations in the aftermath of the financial crisis of 2007-09.

Spain

Spain provides an interesting study. Boasting the fourth-best railroad infrastructure, the country has issues elsewhere. What the WEF considered reckless spending on poorly planned projects has resulted in large debts and several completely empty, unused airports. Not good.

United Kingdom

Our neighbors across the pond enjoy high ranking for electricity supply. On the flip side, the UK ranks 29th in road quality and 19th in air transport infrastructure. Their railroads are expensive yet plagued with delays.

Germany

Germany does well with railroads, ranking ninth, but port infrastructure and electricity come in lower at 14th and 20th, respectively.

Switzerland

Like the US and Germany, Switzerland has seen its infrastructure quality drop since the financial crisis. The Swiss still come in at the top in electricity supply (first) and railroads (second). Their ports, however, ranked 47th, and road quality was ninth.

United Arab Emirates

You might be wondering who has the best road quality. I know I was. Well, it's the United Arab Emirates. They also came in second in air transport infrastructure.

Netherlands

The Netherlands boasts the top spot in port quality, and second in road quality.

Singapore

Singapore tops the list in air transport quality and ranks second in port quality. They drop to 29th in telephone lines and 14th in mobile phone subscriptions.

Hong Kong

Hong Kong is generally regarded as having the best infrastructure in the world. [23]

Our Infrastructure is Getting Wet

Wait, what? Don't the builders know about rain? Well, yes. But what they didn't know was how much precipitation would increase and the extent to which climate change would affect our infrastructure. According to William Becker, a contributor to the Presidential Climate Action Project, the United States saw increases in heavy precipitation between 1958 and 2012 of between 5 percent in the Southwest and a jaw-dropping 71 percent in the northeast. Not to mention the rising water levels that affect many of our bridges and put their structural soundness at risk. This is not cheap stuff to fix, folks. Our government must step up with increased funding. [24]

The US & Germany - A Home Comparison

I want to spend some time comparing and contrasting German building codes and attitudes towards homeownership with those in the US. Here, I probably don't have to tell you about the many, many subdivisions full of practically identical, often inexpensively built homes. You simply don't see these types of subdivisions in Germany, and the homes vary greatly from one to another. Whereas most homes in the US are made of wood, German homes tend to be constructed of brick masonry from a concrete mixture. Interestingly, homeownership is also far less common in Germany, and rent and lease agreements often span years. Most new home construction is intended to rent out.

Of course, each building material has its pros and cons. What the Germans call "Kalksandsteinmauerwerk" (a marvelously Germanesque word for the aforementioned brick masonry) provides excellent insulation but poor Wi-Fi reach (and difficulty in hanging any art). Although nearly ubiquitous here, central heat and air are somewhat rare in German homes. They instead use creative and effective shutters and other more affordable methods of temperature mediation. Kalksandsteinmauerwerk also tends to last (and last), while wooden American homes aren't necessarily built with longevity in mind. This is costly, wasteful, and inefficient. [25]

It may be minor but what I found to be extremely convenient and efficient are the windows in Germany. Every hotel, office building, and home I visited had windows that open two different ways depending on which way you turn the handle. The entire window opens inwards horizontally, and also opens inwards at the top vertically. It's refreshing when in a stuffy hotel room or office building and you just want a little fresh air.

Another significant difference between the US and Germany is roofing materials. Most US homes are built with asphalt shingles and German homes with Slate roofs. Let's look at some pros and cons of both materials. [26]

Asphalt Shingle Pros:
- Low cost
- Easy to install
- Comes in many colors

Asphalt Shingle Cons:
- Lifespan – life expectancy is between 20-30 years
- Less Durability – they are lightweight and are easily damaged by the elements
- Susceptible to extreme weather – high winds can easily tear off shingles and they can warp in the summer and crack in the winter
- Not green – one of the most unfriendly environmental products

Slate Pros:
- Long Life – can last 100-150 years
- Durability – withstands the elements
- Environmentally Friendly – slate is a natural substance or composite of natural substances
- Appearance – adds elegance to homes

Slate Cons:
- Cost – slate costs considerably more
- Weight – slate weighs more and may require additional structural considerations
- Expertise – Requires a higher level of expertise to install

In the US, we tend to go for cheap vs. resilient. In the long run, this ends up costing us more when it comes to repairs or replacement. Our leadership should up the ante when it comes to stricter building codes.

Power Lines

In modern homes, we're pretty much powerless without electricity. With apologies for the bad pun, think back to the last time you lost power for an extended period of time. Life all but grinds to a halt, right? Food spoils, TVs are dark, it's hot (or cold), you can't cook, or take a hot shower, or surf the web, or stay up past sundown without a drove of clunky batteries.

If I asked someone in Germany to think back on their last major power outage, they wouldn't be able to - they simply don't happen. The reason for this is simple: underground power lines. Wind, ice, lightning, and falling trees - the primary culprits in downed lines - aren't an issue when the lines are buried.

Shifting from above ground to below-ground power lines isn't a simple or inexpensive solution in execution, but it is something our leaders should have on their radar. Loss of power is not always just about convenience and creature comforts like television and Wi-Fi. As this part of our infrastructure continues to age and power outages become longer and more common, outages also become more dangerous. Our citizens left to roast in hot summers or freeze in the winters, particularly those with health conditions or dependent on electronic life support equipment, are at a legitimate risk of health complications or even death. [27]

Update – As I am getting ready to publish this book in a couple of weeks, Hurricane Isaias made landfall in North Carolina as a category 1 hurricane on August 5, 2020. The hurricane was downgraded to a tropical storm after making landfall. It was a quick-moving storm and headed straight up the eastern seaboard. It ran through, North Carolina, Virginia, Maryland, Delaware, New Jersey, Pennsylvania, New York, Connecticut, Rhode Island, Massachusetts, Vermont, New Hampshire, and Maine, before heading into Canada.

It is estimated that over 5,315,000 people lost electricity as a result of the storm. I was also one of the over 5 million people that lost power. I consider myself fortunate since I only lost power for 24 hours. It's now five days later and there are still people without power. This was only a tropical storm - could you imagine if it were a category 3, 4, or 5 hurricane? I think it's time to make an investment in underground power lines. What do you think?

Urban Sprawl

When you hear the term "urban sprawl", what comes to mind? SUV-clogged five-lane roads lined with strip centers and chain restaurants?

Neighborhoods packed full of identical houses? A long commute? Urban sprawl is all of that, and it has definite impacts on our environment and economy.

Technically, urban sprawl refers to poorly planned expansions taking up large swaths of land and putting long distances between residential areas and commercial areas. While it can be argued that this type of expansion brings economic benefits, the cons likely outweigh any pros. High water and air pollution, traffic jams and increased accidents, runoff that pollutes streams and rivers, higher taxes, loss of usable land for agriculture and wildlife, and even health impacts such as obesity and related issues all result from urban sprawl. That's a lot! Add in that most of the structures are poorly built and fall into disrepair, vacancies, and general urban blight, and urban sprawl become a real problem.

Why the health complications? A study by Smart Growth America found that those living in areas of urban sprawl were less likely to engage in physical activity such as walking and biking, which leads to weight gain and high blood pressure. In fact, the study found that the likelihood of developing high blood pressure increases six percent for every 50-point increase in the degree of sprawl. Lack of physical activity and high BMI are factors in over 200,000 premature deaths each year. This is a real problem, folks. [28]

So, where does this tendency toward urban sprawl originate? You guessed it - our government. Rather than putting any resources into improving existing communities. tax subsidies are thrown at these new developments, costings millions for new water and sewer lines, new schools, police, and fire protection. All of that means higher taxes for existing residents.

Dependence on our cars is an issue of concern throughout this chapter, and urban sprawl is no different. According to data from the Sierra Club, an average American driver spends 443 hours driving. Yeah. That's a lot of time behind the wheel - sitting. In fact, urban sprawl residents drive three to four times as much as those living in more compact and better-planned communities. More time in the car leads to more pollution, higher body weight, and increased risk of suffering a car accident.

I'm not suggesting that expanding into the suburbs is avoidable. What I am suggesting is that it be done wisely. Planning for how to link a new community with existing services should be well thought out, not slapped together. Mass transit options should be expanded as these communities are planned, therefore reducing dependency on automobiles. Paths and trails should be established, linking the new communities and encouraging physical activity. Schools and emergency services should also be linked, as opposed to starting from scratch each and every time. So basically, I am just saying we should be smart about it.

Smart Cities

Speaking of being smart, let's talk about smart cities. What is a "smart city" exactly? No, I'm not referring to the average IQ in a given town. Have you heard of the Internet of Things (IoT)? How about that Alexa device in your living room? Yep, that's an example of IoT. But what does that have to do with cities? Simple: smart cities use data collected from various IoT sensors to gain insight and make improvements to the overall operations of those cities. Data can be collected from people, buildings, devices and assets and used to monitor and improve services such as traffic and transportation, power and utilities, water and waste management, and crime detection. Libraries and hospitals can also benefit from community data. In fact, when I think of infrastructure and where the US should be investing, I think of smart cities.

Officials running smart cities can better interact with the community and city infrastructure to observe and track how the city is growing and evolving. technological, economic and environmental changes such as climate change, economic restructuring, the coronavirus, online retail and entertainment, aging populations, urban population growth, and pressures on public finances have increased interest in smart cities.[29]

What Can We Learn from Other Countries?

The following article, <u>5 Smart City Examples from Around the Globe</u> from City Innovators, highlights five examples of what cities around the world are doing when it comes to smart city solutions:

There is a lot happening in the world of smart cities right now. In this article, we explore smart city examples from around the world to see how leaders in Athens, Greece, Chennai, India, Buenos Aires, Argentina, Canterbury-Bankstown, Australia, and Prague, Czech Republic are solving city problems with technology and innovation.

Athens, Greece

In 2010-2011, Athens, Greece was facing some major financial problems. The city had huge debt—280 million euros—and a huge deficit as well—45 million euros per year. The local government couldn't hire new staff, and it also had the typical problem of people working in silos instead of collaborating. To add to that, the city was experiencing social problems too. Citizens of Athens did not trust the government, and in 2015-2016, things got even trickier when a flood of 300,000 Syrian refugees came to the city. As Chief Digital Officer of Athens, Konstantinos Champidis, puts it, 'We had the perfect storm.'

Flash forward a few years, and Athens received the award for the 2018 European Capital of Innovation. How did the city manage this huge transformation 'overnight'? Here are some highlights:

Athens went into their smart city endeavors with the mindset that, "A smart city is more than a sum of platforms and investments and tools. It's about how we're going to transform our cities and change our cities. It's about change."

They started out with a solid structure, which included creating a tool kit and a digital roadmap and setting a position for a Chief Digital Officer.

Athens city leaders realized that they couldn't solve all the city problems alone. They formed partnerships with the private sector and universities and enlisted their help in finding and implementing solutions.

They created a living strategy document for 2018. "It was not ambitious or revolutionary, but we did it," says Konstantinos. The strategy focused on solving real problems that real citizens face, including investing in infrastructure and the government, boosting digital skills of the elderly and unemployed, delivering and coordinating support for refugees, and boosting engagement with citizens by creating online platforms.

The city used its private sector and university partnerships to boost trust in the government. Citizens wouldn't have trusted digital skills courses run by the city, so they invited big tech companies and universities to deliver these courses for free. As people saw that the city could create partnerships and solve their problems, trust grew.

"This is a brief story about Athens that started from a debt crisis and ended up as the European Innovation Capital of 2018," says Konstantinos. The city earned that title because it invested not in technology, tools, and platforms, but because it formed partnerships with universities and businesses, and focused on solving real problems of the citizens. [30]

Chennai, India

The city of Chennai, India is experiencing many challenges, but it is tackling these problems one by one using smart city solutions. The list of challenges likely sounds familiar to any city leader: a large population of 8 million, congestion from private cars, poor infrastructure, pollution. Raj Cherubal, Director at Chennai City Connect, gives several examples of the smart city projects underway in Chennai that are aimed at solving these problems:

Improving the livability of the city by adding public spaces, despite opposition that adding public space may destroy business and be the end of the city Chennai is looking to create its own version of Times Square.

Promoting the use of German GPS-enabled bikes to cut down on private cars on the roads. Although people in a developing country may see bicycles as a step backward (when wealth is growing, and one may finally be able to afford a personal car), the city has helped adoption rates by glamorizing these fancy bikes that can be tracked and booked in advance.

Adding infrastructure underground throughout the city. This is difficult because there is not much data on where water pipes are, so Chennai is working on Geographic Information System (GIS) mapping and advanced tunneling technology.

Creating the largest parking management system in the country, if not the world. This camera-based system will be able to recognize empty parking spots on the road; then citizens can use an app to reserve their parking spot in advance.

Setting up smart classrooms. The city has partnered with Samsung to put smart technology in the classrooms. As Raj puts it, this is "the tip of the iceberg" in terms of all the things they may be able to do to make classrooms smarter.

Restoring 3,000 bodies of water, some simple and some complex. This project includes the use of drones that can land on the water's surface, take a sample, analyze it, and send real-time information on pollution levels.

This is just a shortlist of the many projects happening or in the planning stage in Chennai, which also includes solar energy, 3D mapping, digital signs, a data center, and a disaster management center. While the projects will help increase revenue for the city, they are also helping to break down silos within government and increase the quality of life for residents. [30]

Buenos Aires, Argentina

Buenos Aires is the economic and political capital of Argentina, a large city that is being transformed through the smart application of technology. The modernization and innovation strategy was set out in 2007 when the current president of Argentina was elected mayor of Buenos Aires City. "Our innovation strategy has one main focus, and that is to keep improving our citizen's quality of life," explains Matias Williams, Assistant Secretary of Smart City from the Buenos Aires government. The two major focuses of the strategy are to transform public administration and to take a citizen-centered focus in all projects. Here are some examples of the things they have accomplished or are working on in those areas:

The city of Buenos Aires used to have entire offices filled with paper files. In the last two years, they have managed to digitize these files and create two data centers. Going forward, they are trying to keep everything digital whenever possible, including signing executive orders digitally.

Another improvement was a change in the way people contact the government. With 50 offices, if a citizen has a problem, they might be confused as to which office to call. To solve this, the city created a simpler system with a short phone number (147). Now, no matter the question or problem, citizens can call that number. This makes it simpler and also helps improve the perception of the government because it is now presented in a unified way instead of dozens of individual departments.

Knowing the popularity of smartphones and messaging apps, the city also created a program called Digital Citizen that allows individuals to access city services, get notifications and get digital documents. They are also working on creating a ChatBot to deliver this information within the What's App app, considering that 90 percent of Argentinians already have that app on their phone.

To improve public administration, the city of Buenos Aires is also moving from being an intuition-based government to an evidence-based government. For example, they have created a model that will allow them to predict where, when, and how large a school should be in each neighborhood in the city.

The initiatives in Buenos Aires are aimed at improving how the government runs and how citizens experience the city [30].

Canterbury-Bankstown, Australia

Canterbury-Bankstown is a local government located in south-western Sydney, inside the state of New South Wales in Australia. Like other local Australian councils, funding is really limited, and the local government has been disrupted by the shaky federal government for the past few years. Canterbury-Bankstown is also unique in that it is one of the leanest councils in Australia, with fewer staff members as compared to the population served—a population of 373,000 that includes 44 percent of residents who were born overseas, and 60 percent who speak a language other than English.

Here, Patrhyce Donovan, a Canterbury-Bankstown Council board member, discusses the pillars of the council's smart city plan, which they will be moving forward within the months and years to come.

Canterbury-Bankstown is fortunate to have a mayor who supports smart city projects. He has been championing it, which Patrhyce says helps to prioritize the work and drive change.

Patrhyce and her team have put out a smart city roadmap to guide their way. This comprehensive document spells out all the things the local government is promising to do, along with setting priorities and keeping an eye on emerging trends.

To explain the roadmap, Patrhyce says, "At the end of the day, it comes down to three simple things: the people, places, and processes." In its final version, the roadmap will include a fourth element too—policy.

In terms of people, the roadmap is focused on creating an informed and engaged community. This includes building a culture of innovation within the local government. To achieve that, the roadmap decentralizes the organization, making everyone in it empowered to take on change themselves. Thus, the 'people' aspect of the roadmap includes the citizens and the local government, and it is also about bringing in other partnerships and stakeholders.

The roadmap seeks to create smart places too. This includes thinking about how the city uses places and infrastructure, and how places are maintained.

Finally, the roadmap includes the element of smart processes, which means setting up the platforms, plans, policies, and procedures that will allow the city to solve problems and function efficiently. In terms of processes, data is a vital ingredient that will promote continuous improvement within Canterbury-Bankstown.

"My role is empowering people across the organization and leading them through purpose, passion, possibility," says Patrhyce, "Getting them to understand that they can do different things and think a little bit differently, and make real improvements for the customer." [30]

Prague, Czech Republic

The Czech Republic is a country with 10 million people located in central Europe. The capital, Prague, is the largest city in the country and contributes about 30 percent of the economy of the state. Prague faces many of the same challenges experienced by other cities. The city is growing, and those who want to live in the city expect a comfortable life, placing high expectations on everything from housing and transportation to waste management and energy. In Prague, smart city projects are tackled by a separate company that is owned by the state. Here, Pavel Tesar, a representative from that company, discusses how the arrangement works and some of the projects they have worked on.

The state-owned company was established to fulfill the IT and smart city needs of Prague. The advantage is that the company is able to quickly and efficiently work on city requests and doesn't experience budget problems. On the other hand, Pavel says that getting approvals can be difficult because sometimes city organizations don't cooperate well, and the company itself doesn't have a direct decision-making role.

The company has created a policy that internally they call Pipeline. This process management policy helps because it guides ideas to fruition.

The city is currently running 60 projects, some of which have finished and others which are brand new. The work is handled by a group of 120 employees.

The company brings in stakeholders to assist with projects. This includes the economic sphere and also academia. They don't consider themselves to be the 'best brains,' but know that through working with stakeholders, they can have access to the brightest minds in and outside of the country.

The strategy for smart city projects is divided into five areas— mobility, smart buildings, waste-free city, people in the urban environment, and tourism. A sixth area is the data platform, which is the flagship project.

Projects include the previously mentioned data platform, as well as sensor projects to analyze traffic and the environment, a regional transportation ticketing system, and energy monitoring/savings.

Pavel says that any IT or smart city idea that successfully goes through the council is tackled by his team. While they have made progress in many areas, they are still working to find good solutions to other issues, including the need for more charging stations to make electronic mobility work in the city.

These smart city examples paint a picture of what is happening on the ground in smart city initiatives around the globe, where technology and innovation are being used to solve city problems and improve quality of life for citizens. [30]

Singapore

And finally, here is yet another smart city example: <u>Singapore to spend US$1 billion in smart city initiative during 2019</u> by CIO:

Singapore tops the list of cities that will spend the most money on smart city projects, In a new update to its Worldwide Semiannual Smart Cities Spending Guide, IDC forecasts worldwide spending on smart cities initiatives to reach US$95.8 billion in 2019, an increase of 17.7% over 2018. The Asia Pacific (APAC) region represents over 40% of the total global expenditure.

…Under its Smart Nation Initiative, launched in 2014, Singapore has embarked on strategic national projects that reduce friction between the government, businesses and citizens, improving productivity while paying attention to sustainability.

Ranking an impressive 6th position in the top world smart cities 2018 index by the IESE Business School in Barcelona, Singapore is at the forefront of the digital economy, digital government and digital society.

The island nation received the City Award at the Smart City Expo World Congress (SCEWC) 2018 in Barcelona last November. The award recognizes Singapore government's investments in technology and connectivity infrastructure.

Some of the initiatives rolled out within the smart city framework is taking most of the government to the digital realm and implementing e-government services, launching a unified QR code system, or implementing legislation and infrastructure for autonomous vehicles.

Speaking at the SCEWC, Dr. Janil Puthucheary, Minister-in-charge of GovTech, highlighted the need for "transformation through technology".

He added that "the application of these technologies must benefit our grandchildren and re-engineer our country to improve lives for generations to come." [31]

US Smart City Initiatives

Lest you think no American cities are jumping on these innovations, there are some examples right here in the US of cities that have started smart city initiatives. I would say we are far from being able to call them actual smart cities, but it's a start. One of the major obstacles to getting started is funding. There is some federal grant money available, but it is limited. The US Department of Transportation launched a smart city challenge back in 2015, *asking mid-sized cities across America to develop ideas for an integrated, first-of-its-kind smart transportation system that would use data, applications, and technology to help people and goods move more quickly, cheaply, and efficiently.* [32]

Another source of funding, and more promising, is Public-Private Partnerships. In this case, the private funding comes from companies, usually those that have a vested interest. Let's take a look at some of these initiatives:

Las Vegas, Nevada

Las Vegas is currently testing three pilot projects. The city obligated $500 million to find ways to connect the entire city by 2025. One project uses sensors to track traffic patterns and maneuver traffic through streetlights connected by sensors. The project also records the reduction of CO2 emissions that are realized by eliminating congestion. A second pilot that also uses sensors focuses on pedestrian safety. The sensors detect movement in intersections when pedestrians step into crosswalks. If there is a danger of a pedestrian being struck, the sensors change traffic lights to red to stop oncoming traffic. The third pilot is designed to detect when trash receptacles are full and when streetlights are out. This project's objective is to improve maintenance operations in the city. [33]

Portland, Oregon

Portland is using similar IoT technology that attaches a network of sensors to city streetlights and traffic signals. This pilot project provides data about air quality based on improvements made by regulating stalled traffic. If successful, the city will expand the project from major intersections to the city as a whole. The project is supported by a National Institute of Standards and Technology (NIST) Replicable Smart City Technologies Cooperative Agreement grant. The project is a partnership with the Portland Bureau of Transportation, NIST and Portland State University. Three sensor providers contributed three devices each to the project. [33]

Kansas City, Missouri

Kansas City embraced a public-private partnership for its IoT efforts. Municipal officials supplied $3.7 million for the project, and private-sector partners financed another $12.3 million. The project installed 25 kiosks for citizens to connect to the Internet to receive city information. The kiosks where information can be obtained also function as an emergency alert system. The city's repayment model for the initial capital investment will come from advertising revenue that will be incorporated in the programs. The private-sector partner will share in the revenues and has announced that it will likely recoup all its capital costs in less than five years. [33]

New York City

New York City is using smart city solutions to help solve issues such as water quality and conservation, public safety, and waste management. The office of technology and innovation is partnering with private companies to install technologies like automated water meters, smart trash bins, and smart streetlights.

The New York State Department of Transportation (NYSDOT) is offering $3 million dollar funding for projects that can help reduce transportation congestion, encourage energy-friendly transportation modes, and improve overall transportation.

The city is developing a connected vehicle technology solution to minimize crashes and traffic-related deaths. This program equips vehicles with a device that will provide them with real-time data on road conditions. These safety applications alert the driver to help avoid a crash or diminish its impact. [34]

I'll discuss this more in the economics chapter, but in my opinion, we need to make more of a concerted effort to drive smart city initiatives and other infrastructure initiatives further. Similar to how President Eisenhower put in place the Federal-Aid Highway Act in 1956, to connect the interstate highways across the US, we should be developing plans for how we implement (connect) smart city technology and other technologies across the

US. We should avoid different solutions and technologies. This will allow for compatibility, integration, and interoperability across cities as well as a similar user experience when traveling from one city to another.

There will always be a place for private partnerships, but we should increase federal funding as well. If we look at one of the key elements that lifted the country out of the Great Depression, it was investing in infrastructure.

Charity – Built for Zero

"Built for Zero is a methodology, a movement, and proof of what is possible. The movement is made up of more than 80 cities and counties that have committed to measurably ending homelessness, one population at a time. Using data, these communities have changed how local homeless response systems work and the impact they can achieve.

Twelve of those communities have ended homelessness for a population by reaching a standard called Functional Zero. More than half of those cities and counties have achieved reductions in the number of people experiencing chronic and veteran homelessness.

Together, they are proving that moral courage, data-driven thinking, and a system-wide approach can build a future where homelessness is rare overall and brief when it occurs."

Website - community.solutions/our-solutions/built-for-zero

CHAPTER 4 – HEALTHCARE

"When you have your health, you have everything. When you do not have your health, nothing else matters at all"
- Augusten Burroughs – Author

"He who has health, has hope; he who has hope, has everything"
- Arabian Proverb

Does it seem to you like the debate about healthcare in our country goes on and on and gets uglier and uglier, while the care we receive gets worse and our costs go up? Yeah. Me too. It's not just your imagination though: plenty of evidence backs up this perception. [35]

Where Do We Rank?

The 2014 Commonwealth Fund Survey compared the United States with France, Australia, Germany, Canada, Sweden, New Zealand, Norway, the Netherlands, Switzerland and the UK. [36] Guess where we ranked? When it comes to efficiency, equity, and outcomes, we came in 11th of 11, while at the same time paying more than anyone else. Clearly something is broken here.

The report noted that the key difference between the United States and these 10 other industrialized nations was our lack of universal healthcare. Will we ever get there? Your guess is as good as mine. I'm not optimistic. And, although the Commonwealth Survey is a few years old now, does anyone think things have gotten better? I didn't think so. The Affordable Care Act (Obamacare) has made a few important strides but is heavily flawed and not adequately addressing our problems.

	UK	SWI	SWE	AUS	GER	NETH	NZ	NOR	FRA	CAN	US
OVERALL RANKING	1	2	3	4	5	5	7	7	9	10	11
Quality Care	1	3	10	2	7	5	4	11	8	9	5
Access	1	2	4	8	2	4	7	6	11	9	9
Efficiency	1	6	2	4	9	7	3	4	8	10	11
Equity	2	2	1	5	4	8	10	6	7	9	11
Healthy Lives	10	3	2	4	7	5	9	6	1	8	11
Health Expenditure/Capita	$3,405	$5,643	$3,925	$3,800	$4,495	$5,099	$3,182	$5,669	$4,118	$4,522	$8,508

Source: www.commonwealthfund.org mirror mirror on the wall

US Life Expectancy

Better healthcare leads to a healthier and longer lifespan, right? Theoretically yes, and there certainly are Americans who can afford high quality healthcare and are living longer. But let's take a closer look at one of the areas where we ranked dead last among those 11 countries: equity.

If I asked you what countries have the highest life expectancy, you'd probably guess that we do here in the United States. And in some places, that's true. It's a good guess.

But here's a sobering statistic: In certain regions of our country, life expectancy can't even match some third-world countries. That's right – the life expectancy is higher in Iraq, the Philippines, and North Korea than it is in certain counties in South and North Dakota. (Yes, you read that right. I know – I was surprised too.) [37] Now, that might not be a nationwide statistic, but I, for one, am not okay with any county in the United States having a lower life expectancy than some third-world country. I'm guessing you aren't either.

In a study conducted by the Institute for Health Metrics and Evaluation at the University of Washington, Seattle, in 2017, life expectancy and mortality rates were tracked by county across the United States and compared to statistics from 1980. Not surprisingly, overall, Americans are living longer. But – and this is a big but – where some areas had seen big surges in how long people are living, some areas had actually seen a reduction in life expectancy. The disparity between the highest and lowest is a whopping 20 years.

One of the study's authors noted the inequality of the American healthcare system as a major factor in the findings, and that big changes are needed at all levels of government health departments.

Infant Mortality Rate

In an article by Andy East, <u>Why is the infant mortality rate in the United States so high?</u> The author notes that *While infant mortality rates around the world have dramatically decreased over the past decades, data shows the US isn't keeping pace, particularly with other highly-developed nations around the world.*

The U.S infant mortality rate in 1960 was 25.9 deaths per 1,000 live births, the 12th lowest in the world, according to the United Nations Interagency Group for Child Mortality Estimation, which compiles data for the World Health Organization and UNICEF.

By 1980, the US rate had dropped to 15.9 deaths per 1,000 live births, but that was only 18th lowest in the world. And in 1990, the US rate was 9.4 per 1,000 live births, still dropping, but now the 26th lowest in the world.

That means that most developed countries in the world are surpassing the US in lowering the infant death rate more quickly than our own.

The infant mortality rate in most developed countries in 2017 — such as Japan, Iceland, Sweden, Austria, South Korea, Italy, France, Sweden, among several others — tended to hover at around 2 to 3.5 deaths per 1,000 live births, or approximately two to three times less than the US rate.

In 2017, 54 countries had a lower infant mortality rate than the US, according to the Central Intelligence Agency's World Factbook, which compiles a wide range of data on countries around the world for use by US government officials. The US rate in 2017 was 5.8, which was tied with Serbia, just a hair higher than Bosnia and Herzegovina, which had a rate of 5.5, and slightly lower than Qatar, which had a rate of 6.2.

Japan had the lowest rate of any country — 2 deaths per 1,000 live births. The infant mortality rate in Hong Kong, which is often listed as a separate country than mainland China, was 2.7, or roughly half the US rate. Cuba, the Communist island nation just south of Florida, had a rate of 4.4.

The infant mortality rate in the US, however, is far from uniform. Data from the federal Centers for Disease Control show a wide disparity among all 50 states and the District of Columbia in 2017, ranging from 8.6 deaths per 1,000 live births in Mississippi to 3.7 deaths per 1,000 live births in Massachusetts.

Indiana, for its part, had an infant mortality rate in 2017 of 7.3 deaths per 1,000 live births — the seventh highest rate in the country. Only Mississippi, Arkansas, Oklahoma, South Dakota, Alabama and Tennessee had higher rates. The rate in Indiana was 9.5 in 1990 and 7.5 in 2000.

If the Hoosier state was a country, it would have had the 64th lowest infant mortality rate in the world in 2017 — sandwiched between Kuwait and Lebanon on the list.

…While not all causes of infant death are preventable — the United States as a whole, and particularly Indiana, tends to fare poorly in many measures of public health and social determinants considered risk factors for infant mortality.

"A healthier mom leads to a healthier pregnancy and a healthier baby," said Dr. Tracey Wilkinson, assistant professor at the Indiana University School of Medicine, licensed pediatrician and board member at Physicians for Reproductive Health.

Indiana ranked 41st out of 50 states in United Health Foundation's 2018 America's Health Rankings, including 44th in smoking, 39th in obesity, 40th in diabetes, 26th in low birth weight and 29th in child poverty.

Additionally, Indiana ranked 27th in uninsured residents and 48th in public health funding, spending approximately $51 per capita in combined state and federal funding in 2017 and 2018. Alaska spent the most of any state, $281 per capita. The US average was $86. The March of Dimes estimates that preterm births cost Indiana $417 million each year in medical costs, lost wages and lost productivity.

"When you don't invest in public health, your outcomes are not going to be good," Wilkinson said.

In 2017, 47.3 percent of infant deaths in Indiana were attributed to perinatal risks (from 22 weeks of gestation until one year after birth), 18.1 percent to congenital malformations (birth defects), and 16.6 percent to SUIDs, or the sudden unexpected infant death, according to the Indiana State Department of Health.

Perinatal risks typically are "health conditions caused by being born too early and too sick," said Jeena Siela, director of maternal child health and government affairs for March of Dimes in Indiana.

"If we could address preterm birth, we could significantly reduce infant mortality," Siela said.

Some of the factors that directly related to prematurity and low birth weight that are preventable include smoking and appropriately spaced pregnancies, which refers to how soon the mother should wait after one pregnancy before getting pregnant again, said Wilkinson, who typically advises mothers to wait 18 to 24 months between pregnancies. Obesity is another factor that directly relates to preterm birth and low birth weight, she said.

"The strongest predictor for a healthy pregnancy is a planned pregnancy, and Indiana has one of the highest rates of unplanned pregnancies," Wilkinson said. About half of pregnancies in the United States are unplanned, according to the Centers for Disease Control.

The smoking rate in Indiana also is relatively high among pregnant women. Around 13.5 percent of women in Indiana smoke during their pregnancy, according to the Indiana State Department of Health. The national rate is 12.6 percent. In 2018, 18 percent, or nearly one in five, of women who gave birth at Columbus Regional Hospital reported smoking during their pregnancy, according to Kylene Jones, tobacco awareness coordinator at Healthy Communities and CRH.

Approximately one in three Hoosiers, or 33.6 percent, were obese in 2017, according to the State Health Access Data Assistance Center, a multidisciplinary health policy research center affiliated with the University of Minnesota. Obesity is defined as having a body mass index greater than 30. In 1990, Indiana's obesity rate was 13.3 percent, according to the State of Obesity, an annual report by Washington, D.C.-based non-profit Trust for America's Health and the Robert Wood Johnson Foundation, a public health philanthropy based in New Jersey.

In 2014, the state of Indiana released a report that looked at potential ways to reduce infant mortality in the state to reach its goal of a statewide infant mortality rate of 4.5 deaths per 1,000 live births.

The report found that "infant mortality risk in the state of Indiana is not randomly distributed, but exhibits statistically significant patterns that could be used for targeted investment of resources to improve outcomes." Not getting adequate prenatal care, young age of the mother and being enrolled in Medicaid were among the biggest predictors of "adverse birth outcomes," according to the report.

Infant mortality is "a tough thing to fix," Siela said. "You're talking about system changes, insurance changes. At the end of the day, this is a societal issue. Infant mortality is a huge lens into the health of a nation." [44]

Again, I ask you, why should the United States trail in such a basic and yet vital category? The answer is, it shouldn't.

The Need for Single-Payer Universal Health Care

The United States does have a few variations on Universal Health Care, including Medicaid, Medicare, Children's Health Insurance Program, and Veterans military coverage. Through the Affordable Care Act, the government subsidizes private health insurance. Over 67 percent of Americans have private health insurance, mostly through our employers. [39]

	Country	Type	% of GDP	Per Capita	Wait 4+ weeks	Infant Mortality Rate (2017)
Universal Healthcare Comparison						
	Australia	2-tier	9.6%	$4,798	22%	3.0
	Canada	Single	10.6%	$4,752	56.3%	4.5
	France	2-tier	11.0%	$4,600	49.3%	3.5
	Germany	Mandate	11.3%	$5,550	11.9%	3.1
	Singapore	2-tier	4.9%	$2,000	-	2.2
	Switzerland	Mandate	12.4%	$7,919	20.2%	3.7
	UK	Single	9.7%	$4,193	29.9%	3.7
	USA	Private	18.0%	$9,892	4.9%	5.7

Source: www.thebalance.com/universal-health-care-4156211

A recent study, published in The Lancet Medical Journal, estimates that more than 37 million Americans do not have health insurance, and another 41 million have inadequate access to care. Based on the table above, the United States has the highest spend on healthcare per capita.

The study also estimates that a single-payer universal health care system could lead to a 13 percent savings in national health care costs, which is roughly equivalent to US$450 billion per year (let's keep that in mind for chapter 7 on the Economy). In addition, the study estimates that providing health care access for all Americans would save more than 68,000 lives. [40]

What Can We Learn from Other Countries?

Australia

Australia has a mixed health plan. The government provides public health insurance, called Medicare, and runs public hospitals. Everyone receives coverage. People must pay deductibles before government payments kick in. Many residents are willing to pay for additional private health insurance to receive a higher quality of care. Government regulations protect seniors, the poor, children, and rural residents.

In 2018, health care cost 9.3% of Australia's gross domestic product. That's fairly low. The per capita cost was US$5,005, about average for developed countries. There were 42.6% of patients who reported a wait time of more than four weeks to see a specialist. Australia had one of the best infant mortality rates of the compared countries at 3.1% [40]

Canada

Canada has a national health insurance system. The government pays for services provided by a private delivery system. Private supplemental insurance pays for vision, dental care, and prescription drugs. Hospitals are publicly funded. They provide free care to all residents regardless of their ability to pay. The government keeps hospitals on a fixed budget to control costs but reimburses doctors at a fee-for-service rate.

In 2018, health care cost 10.7% of Canada's GDP. The cost per person was US$4,974 a whopping 62.8% of patients waited more than four weeks to see a specialist. The infant mortality rate was 4.3%. [40]

France

France has a social health insurance system that provides care to all legal residents. That includes hospitals, doctors, medications and some dental and vision care. It also pays for homeopathy, spa treatments, and nursing home care. Of that, payroll taxes fund 64%, income taxes pay for 16%, and 12% is from tobacco and alcohol taxes.

In 2018, health care cost 11.2% of GDP. That was US$4,965 per person. Half of all patients reported a wait time of more than four weeks to see a specialist. The infant mortality rate was 3.4%. These statistics are all in the middle of the pack for developed nations. [40]

Germany

Germany has a social health insurance program. Everyone must have public health insurance, but those above a certain income can choose private insurance instead. The state-sponsored insurance covers hospitalization, except for meals and accommodation. It also covers rehab for hospital stays, mental health, and addiction. It even covers long-term care. Funding comes from payroll taxes.

In 2018, health care cost 11.2% of GDP. It averaged US$5,986 per person. Both figures are about average. Only 28.1% of patients reported a wait time of more than four weeks to see a specialist. That is among the lowest of the developed countries. In addition, most Germans can get next-day or same-day appointments with general practitioners. The infant mortality rate was 3.1%. [40]

Switzerland

The country has a social health insurance system for all residents. Coverage is provided by competing private insurance companies. Residents pay premiums up to 8% of their income. The government reimburses them for any higher costs. People can buy supplemental insurance to access better hospitals, doctors, and amenities.

In 2018, health care spending was 12.2% of GDP. It was USD $7,317 per person. Only 27.3% of patients reported a wait time of more than four weeks to see a specialist. The infant mortality rate was 3.7%. [40]

United Kingdom

The United Kingdom has single-payer health care that covers all residents. Visitors receive care for emergencies and infectious diseases. The National Health Service runs hospitals and pays doctors as employees. The government pays 80% of costs through income and payroll taxes. The rest is paid from copayments and people paying out-of-pocket for NHS services. It pays for all medical care, including some dental and eye care, hospice care, and some long-term care. There are some copays for prescription drugs. In 2015, 10.5% of U.K. residents had private insurance for elective medical procedures.

In 2018, health care costs were 9.8% of GDP. The cost was US $4,069 per person. But 46.4% of patients reported a wait time of more than four weeks to see a specialist. The infant mortality rate was 3.6%. [40]

Lobbying – "Big Pharma"

Did you know that federal law currently prohibits the Secretary of Health and Human Services from negotiating lower prescription drug prices for Medicare Part D subscribers? In 2019, Medicare Part D spent $62 billion on prescription drugs for the elderly. The Secretary is allowed to negotiate drug prices for other government programs, like Medicaid and Veterans Affairs.

The Congressional Budget Office estimates if the Secretary were allowed to require brand-name drug manufacturers to lower the price of their drugs, Medicare Part D could save $11 billion per year. (let's keep that in mind for chapter 7 on the Economy). [41]

The pharmaceutical industry holds the title as the top lobbying force in Washington. Combined, the pharmaceutical/health products industry, spent $228 million through the third quarter of 2019. [42]

Whose best interests do our politicians put first: the elderly and the need to drive down prescription drug costs, or the large pharmaceutical companies who line their pockets?

As I was getting ready to publish this book, it was announced that President Trump signed four new Executive Orders around pharmaceutical pricing. Part of the problem with writing a book that covers current affairs is that you are never done. Every day I read something relevant to one of the topics in this book and say to myself, "I should add that in!" Obviously, I have to stop at some point. Anyway, back to the Executive Orders.

There is uncertainty as to whether these Executive Orders will actually be implemented since there are a few caveats that must be sorted out.

The first Executive Order has given the drug manufacturers a one-month ultimatum to come up with ways to lower drug prices. [43]

The second Executive Order would eliminate the rebates that drug manufacturers pay to insurers. The caveat here is that it will not be allowed to be implemented if it raises premiums. Early estimates from government actuaries are that this order will increase premiums by up to 25 percent. [43]

The third Executive Order would allow Americans to import medications from other countries, something not allowed in the past. [43]

The fourth Executive Order would require certain health centers to pass negotiated discounts on insulin and EpiPens to patients. Having kids with allergies, I can tell you firsthand that EpiPens are extremely expensive (over $100 each) and you need multiple EpiPens for each child, one in school, one at home, one in the car, etc. [43]

Many people are arguing that Trump has signed these Executive Orders as a last-ditch effort for the upcoming elections in November. In my opinion, I don't care. If it helps lower the costs and gets medications to the people who need them, then it's a good thing.

The Need for Centralized Electronic Health Records

Have you ever shown up for an appointment with a new doctor or specialist, only to spend the first half-hour filling out paperwork you've filled out dozens of times before? Or wondered why you're answering questions about your ears if you're at the proctologist? What if you forgot one when making a list of all the prescriptions you currently take?

It is also frustrating when switching doctors that we must have our records copied from the prior doctor and sent to the new doctor. When applying for life insurance, disability insurance, long-term care, etc. – we have to complete the questionnaires again and then they have to be underwritten over and over again. Certainly seems inefficient, doesn't it?

Folks, we must establish Electronic Health Records (EHR). Now, I get it, these situations described above are at best annoying and at worst infuriating, but a lack of centralized information can have far more dire consequences than just a little lost time at an appointment.

Imagine you're traveling, enjoying your wonderful vacation when illness strikes you or someone you're with, and someone needs to see a doctor. There's currently no efficient way for healthcare professionals to communicate in these types of situations. If you're incapacitated and the college buddies you're reuniting with don't know you're allergic to Penicillin, or you forgot to mention it to an ER doc, well, I don't have to spell out what could happen next.

The Health Insurance Portability and Accountability Act (HIPAA), which protects our personal health information, was actually put in place to set the stage for health and health insurance information to be easily but securely accessible as you go from one provider to another. Yet, ironically, it is what is preventing the sharing of this data. I get that. I'm all for privacy too. But maintaining digital records in an anonymous way can and should be done. Besides – what's more important: your privacy or a doctor knowing not to give you Penicillin?

Okay, here's the truth. I know setting this up won't be easy. But the system (if it can even be called a "system") we have today is just not working.

What Can We Learn from Other Countries?

It's relatively easy to implement something if you're a smaller country versus a larger country. I understand that different countries face different challenges when it comes to nationalizing anything. That said, while no country big or small can boast total EHR implementation, a few are impressively close and are coming up with new ways of converting millions of pieces of paper electronically into one database.

Here is some information on eight countries who have started this process and how they went about starting. [45]

Australia

Initial trial runs of Australia's Shared Electronic Health Record system started back in 2004, working out the many bugs that came up in real-world testing. [45]

As of 2018, more than six million Australians have an Electronic Health Record and 13,956 healthcare professional organizations are connected. This includes general practices, hospitals, pharmacies, diagnostic imaging and pathology practices. Australia is also only one of two countries that allow individuals to edit or author parts of their health records. [49]

Canada

In Western Canada, Alberta Netcare is the province's public EHR system, and allows authorized physicians across the province to view medical records. In turn, the government of Alberta is poised to offer the province's 4 million residents access to their own electronic health records, according to the Canadian Medical Association Journal.

Meanwhile, in Ontario, and after a start-up plagued by delays and a financial scandal, eHealth Ontario is rolling-out an electronic health record system for regional communities. "There's really no comparison to the way we used to do things," Kitchener physician Mel Cescon told apple.com (His clinic now uses a handful of Macs to work with records for 12,000 patients that used to take up several tons of file cabinets.) "The system is so much more efficient. It lets us be better doctors." [45]

Estonia

In 2008, Estonia became the first country in the world to implement a nationwide "birth-to-death" electronic health record system for nearly every citizen. (That was 12 years ago, by the way.) [45]

Denmark

Denmark has a centralized electronic database of its citizens' medical records going back as far as 1977 for basic records, and back as far as 2000 for detailed histories. Approximately 98 percent of primary care physicians have access to the system, including all hospital physicians and all pharmacists. Time Magazine has called the system "a lesson for the US" [45]

Finland

First strategized in 1996, Finnish healthcare professionals and patients now have access to a state-wide EHR system that offers secure information for both healthcare professionals and patients.

The key to Finland's success was careful planning and swift action: Bills in 2006 were passed into law in 2007 with few-to-no bumps along the way. All planned e-health services for the country were online by 2010, and in 2011, it became mandatory for all healthcare professionals to use the system. [45]

The Netherlands

Let's look at another example of where a carefully crafted "let's just get it done" approach worked - without offending anyone or infringing on civil liberties: In 2009, the Dutch minister for youth pushed to make it mandatory to add electronic health records to existing data for all children and their families.

Success here came in a three-step process that involved digitizing existing health records, data transfer, and later, a feasibility study to understand the information exchange chain in children's health care. [45]

Sweden

The Swedish Government recently implemented stage 1 of the Swedish National Patient Summary Initiative – one of the first of its kind in the world.

After just one year developing the legal context, patient consent and IT infrastructure, the nationwide system was rolled-out into a test of more than 300,000 people.

The country enlisted the help of Finland-based Tieto for development, implementation, and hosting, and, get this: Cambridge, Massachusetts-based InterSystems' HealthShare as the health information exchange software program. [45]

United Arab Emirates

While it hasn't implemented electronic health records across the UAE, Abu Dhabi is leading the way in using national EHR information to assess the risk of cardiovascular disease. [45]

A Few Other Thoughts on Centralized Records

Anxiety and Our Youth

- 1 in 5 adults in America experience mental illness. [46]
- 1 in 25 (10 million) adults in America live with a serious mental illness. [46]
- 18.1% (42 million) of American adults live with anxiety disorders. [46]
- Depression is the leading cause of disability worldwide and is a major contributor to the global burden of disease. [46]
- Serious mental illness costs America $193.2 billion in lost earnings every year. [47]
- Suicide is the 10th leading cause of death in the US [47]
- One-half of all chronic mental illness begins by the age of 14; three-quarters by age of 24. [46]

- Among teens 15 to 19, the suicide rate was 8 per 100,000 people in 2000 and then increased to 11.8 per 100,000 in 2017. [48]
- Among young adults 20 to 24, the suicide rate was 12.5 per 100,000 people in 2000 and then rose to 17 per 100,000 in 2017. [48]

Seems like everyone I talk to these days has a kid who struggles with anxiety, depression, or both. Each case is treated individually, and in many cases, the kids are prescribed a high-powered drug. This is a band-aid. It's not getting to the root cause, and, quite frankly, this many kids on anxiety meds scares me for our future.

I personally believe that centralized, digital records could A) bring this anxiety epidemic to light, and B) perhaps correlate the data to get at the root cause.

Mental Health and Gun Control

I talk some about the mental health issues that tie into the gun control debate in another chapter. Imagine how much easier it would be to monitor the purchase and ownership of guns if we had this kind of centralized health records database?

When applying for a gun permit, access to the Centralized Electronic Health Records will determine if the applicant has any history of mental illness, and if so, the request gets denied. The gun shop owner or employees do not need to know why the application was denied. The application process would also determine if there are any other residents at the same address who have any history of mental illness, and again, the application would be denied.

The opposite is true also: if a current gun owner enters treatment for mental illness, or a resident at the same address as the gun owner enters treatment for mental illness, then local law enforcement would automatically receive an alert, and would be required to collect the gun(s) and keep them in safe storage until the situation changes.

To wrap up: It's our health, folks. Our leaders need to do better.

Charity – Jed Foundation

"JED is a nonprofit that protects emotional health and prevents suicide for our nation's teens and young adults. We're partnering with high schools and colleges to strengthen their mental health, substance misuse, and suicide prevention programs and systems. We're equipping teens and young adults with the skills and knowledge to help themselves and each other. We're encouraging community awareness, understanding and action for young adult mental health.."

Website - www.jedfoundation.org/who-we-are

"An investment in education pays the best interest."
- Benjamin Franklin

"Education is the most powerful weapon which you can use to change the World."
- Nelson Mandela

When it comes to preparing future generations to take on and run the country (hopefully better than we are now), few things rank higher in importance than education. A solid education opens doors and creates opportunities that can't be found through other means. Our country is failing our students on several fronts, from falling test scores for middle and high school students to the crippling debt we allow or even encourage our 18-year-olds to take on without any knowledge of what that debt means for their future. We rank well in the percentage of students who go on to pursue higher education, but for those students who come out of college with debt equal to a mortgage and no asset to sell, well, was it worth it?

But first, let's talk about test scores for our high school students. Ask yourself, where do you think we rank globally? I'd like to think we're top 5, or at least the top 10. And we were, at one point. In 1990, the United States' education system ranked sixth in the world according to Business Insider [50]. Although exactly where we rank today varies (sometimes widely) by the testing agency, and the perception globally seems to be that our education system is high quality, the numbers are not something to cheer about. One index, based on research from Pearson.com, ranked the US at 14th of 40 countries in 2014, just behind Russia and just ahead of Australia. South Korea topped that list, followed by Japan, Singapore, and Hong Kong. Asian countries consistently perform well in educational studies. [51]

2015 data from the Program for International Student Assessment (PISA), which tests 15-year-olds from 71 countries in science, math and reading proficiency, puts our students at 24th in reading and science, and an embarrassing 39th in math. In reading and science, the US is at least not worsening (although we're not improving either) and ranks above the global average. In math, however, our 15-year-olds are below average and falling. [61] We must improve this.

Why those numbers are what they are, is, of course, complicated. The Organization for Economic Cooperation and Development (OECD) data confirm that the US is not adept at helping lower-income students thrive in the classroom, and this affects our scores. Our scores are also affected by our lax attitude toward recruiting, training, and paying high-quality teachers. Combating poverty and addressing the lack of qualified people pursuing teaching jobs could go a long way in improving our scores.

Rank	Country	Total Score	Reading Score	Math Score	Science Score
1	China	1731	556	600	575
2	Hong Kong	1637	533	555	549
3	Finland	1631	536	541	554
4	Singapore	1630	526	562	542
5	Japan	1588	520	529	539
6	Canada	1580	524	527	529
7	New Zealand	1572	521	519	532
8	Taiwan	1558	495	543	520
9	Netherlands	1556	508	526	522
10	Australia	1556	515	514	527
11	Liechtenstein	1555	499	536	520
12	Switzerland	1552	501	534	517
13	Estonia	1541	501	512	528
14	Germany	1530	497	513	520
15	Belgium	1528	506	515	507
16	Poland	1503	500	495	508
17	Iceland	1503	500	507	496
18	Norway	1501	503	498	500
19	United Kingdom	1500	494	492	514
20	Denmark	1497	495	503	499
21	Slovenia	1496	483	501	512
22	Ireland	1491	496	487	508
23	France	1491	496	497	498
24	**United States**	**1489**	**500**	**487**	**502**
25	Hungary	1487	494	490	503
26	Sweden	1486	497	494	495
27	Czech Republic	1471	478	493	500
28	Portugal	1469	489	487	493
29	Slovakia	1464	477	497	490
30	Latvia	1460	484	482	494

Source: U.S. NEWS-Best Countries for Education

So, what are we spending on education for these less-than-stellar results? Although spending has fallen some since 2010, we still spend more per student than in many countries. According to OECD, the US spent $16,268 per student from elementary school through post-secondary education in 2014, well above the global average of $10,759. [52]

What Can We Learn from Other Countries?

As Dominic Rushe points out in his article The <u>US spends more on education than other countries. Why is it falling behind?</u> Even though the US is spending more on average than other countries, *"that money does not appear to be translating into better results for US students. According to the Washington thinktank the National Center on Education and the Economy (NCEE), the average student in Singapore is 3.5 years ahead of her US counterpart in math, 1.5 years ahead in reading and 2.5 in science. Children in countries as diverse as Canada, China, Estonia, Germany, Finland, Netherland, New Zealand and Singapore consistently outrank their US counterparts on the basics of education."* [52] What can we learn from these other countries?

Canada

Canada has a lot in common with its larger southern neighbor but has consistently outranked it on education. In Ontario, which educates 40% of Canada's students, nearly 30% of the province's population are immigrants. According to the 2015 Pisa exam results, Ontario scored fifth in the world in reading. Children of immigrants perform compatibly with their peers with Canadian-born parents in educational achievement.

In 2013 teacher training was revamped – lengthening training and reducing the number of slots available in order to improve quality. Decision-making is local but there is a national focus on personalized learning, flexibility and high standards. [52]

Singapore

Fifty years ago the majority of Singapore's population was illiterate; today it is held up as one of the models for education around the world. The island nation, population just 5.6 million, consistently tops world rankings for education.

Education is highly centralized and becoming a teacher is extremely competitive. Candidates are recruited from the top third of secondary school graduates, and less than a fifth of applicants are admitted.

The teacher turnover rate is below 3%, less than half the rate in the US.

In Singapore teachers spend about 40% of their time with students, far less than in the US. The rest of their time is spent on research, lesson planning, and strategizing with other teachers to ensure that their pupils' needs are being met. [52]

Finland

Getting into a teacher training course in Finland is tough. Acceptance rates for the University of Helsinki's teacher education program (6.8%) were lower than its law program (8.3%) and medical school (7.3%) in 2016.

The Finns are committed to keeping their edge in education. Every four years, the government re-evaluates its education plan in order to adapt it to the changing needs of the country. [52]

Germany

In 2000 Germany suffered "Pisa shock". The OECD found German students were below average on core subjects and that the less well-off were suffering far higher rates of educational failure. The report sparked a national debate and government action. New academic standards were brought in, national tests were instituted and more funding went to early learning and immigrant families.

While problems remain – student performance for those further down the socio-economic scale is still lower than the OECD average – Germany's system has shown marked improvements. [52]

South Korea

When Japanese occupation of Korea ended in 1945, it took its teachers with it. Only Japanese nationals had been allowed to teach and attend its secondary schools and higher education institutions and some 80% of the population was illiterate. Today South Korea has one of the world's best-educated populations: in 2015, 69% of 25- to 34-year-olds had completed post-secondary education, the highest rate among all the OECD countries.

South Korea's school system is highly centralized and highly test driven. Teaching is the country's most popular profession and teachers are well paid and highly qualified. Teaching has a clear career path in South Korea and teachers are rewarded for developing their skills. While the starting salary for teachers is slightly below the OECD average of $32,202, at the top of the salary scale teachers make $55,122, higher than the OECD average and more than twice the country's average household income of $21,723 a year. [52]

Some observations on these top performing countries; One, we have to make more of investment in our educators. Being a teacher should be as competitive as being an attorney or a doctor. Two, we need to make sure that our teachers are highly qualified and highly compensated with incentive-laden contracts.

Cost of an Education

When it comes to higher education, the costs in our country are bloated and only getting worse. The average cost per year for the tuition of a public university in the US is pushing $10,000. If you want a private education, you're looking at an average annual tuition fee of $30,000 or more, and many students are graduating with a crippling debt burden. Nearly 15 percent of loan-holders enter the working world owing $50,000 or more. [53] As of 2020, there are 45 million borrowers who collectively owe nearly $1.6 trillion in student loan debt. In fact, student loan debt is now the second-highest consumer debt category - behind only mortgage debt.

Think back for a minute to your 18th birthday. Would you have understood the future implications of taking on that type of debt? I don't think I would have. For students who simply want to attend the college of their choice and for whom four years still feels like an eternity, student loans seem like a no-brainer. They'll get a good job and everything will be fine, right? Then reality hits when that first bill comes due. We're seeing huge numbers of "boomerang" kids moving back home to save money, delaying first home purchases and retirement savings. Our college graduates are starting from less than zero.

An OECD study of 28 countries confirmed that our college costs are the highest in the world. Some countries, including Denmark, Germany, Estonia and Finland, provide free tuition at public universities. Many, such as Austria, Italy, Hungary, and the Netherlands, cost less than $4,000 per year for public institutions, some less than $1,000. Countries on the higher side include Japan at an average of $5,229 and Chile at $7,654. [53]

Average annual tuition fee at a public college		
Rank	Country	Cost
1	Denmark	$0
2	Estonia	$0
3	Finland	$0
4	Germany	$0
5	Norway	$0
6	Poland	$0
7	Slovak Republic	$0
8	Slovenia	$0
9	Sweden	$0
10	Turkey	$0
11	Mexico	$527
12	Luxembourg	$680
13	Hungary	$766
14	Austria	$914
15	Switzerland	$1,168
16	Portugal	$1,472
17	Italy	$1,658
18	Spain	$1,830
19	Netherlands	$2,420
20	Isreal	$3,095
21	Latvia	$3,337
22	New Zealand	$4,295
23	South Korea	$4,578
24	Australia	$4,763
25	Canada	$4,939
26	Japan	$5,229
27	Chile	$7,654
28	**United States**	**$9,960**

Source: Cost-of-college-countries-around-the-world
Insider.com

The US would do well to learn from other countries whose college costs are manageable (or even free!). We can even look in our own backyard: The State University of New York (SUNY) and the City University of New York (CUNY) implemented a new program in 2017 that allows families and individuals making up to $125,000 per year to qualify to attend college tuition-free. [54] I believe more public institutions should follow New York's lead.

We'd also do well by our young folks to teach them about the burdensome effects of debt on their future financial freedom and stability, and counsel them on other options. We must do better for our future generations.

Charity – Jack Kent Cooke Foundation

"The Jack Kent Cooke Foundation is dedicated to advancing the education of exceptionally promising students who have financial need. Since 2000, the Foundation has awarded over $200 million in scholarships to over 2,700 students from 8th grade through graduate school, along with comprehensive educational advising and other support services. The Foundation has also provided $110 million in grants to organizations that serve such students."

Website - www.jkcf.org/about-us

CHAPTER 6 - GUN CONTROL

"It is not the strongest of the species that survives, nor the most intelligent that survives. It is the one that is most adaptable to change."
- Charles Darwin

In the middle of writing this chapter on gun control, two more mass shootings took place within 24 hours of each other: At a Wal Mart in El Paso, Texas, 22 people were killed and 24 injured with an AK 47; In Dayton, Ohio, 9 people were killed and 27 injured in the space of about thirty seconds. That shooter used a high-capacity rifle that holds 250 rounds when fully loaded.

Let's ponder some points: Both of these guns were legal at the time these tragedies occurred. But it wasn't always that way. And it shouldn't be that way. Let's take a look at some US Statistics:

- Over 36,000 Americans are killed by guns each year—an average of 100 per day.[55]
- 100,000 Americans are shot and injured each year [56]
- Of the 36,383 Americans killed with guns each year,[57] 22,274 are gun suicides (61%), 12,830 are gun homicides (35%), 496 are law enforcement shootings (1.4%), and 487 are unintentional shootings (1.3%) [58]
- The United States accounts for just 4% of the world's population but 35% of global firearm suicides and 9% of global firearm homicides [58]
- The US gun homicide rate is 25 times that of other high-income countries [59]
- The US gun suicide rate is 10 times that of other high-income countries [60]
- Women in the United States are 21 times more likely to be murdered with a gun than women in other high-income countries [60]
- Black children are 10 times more likely to be killed in a gun homicide than white children [60]

- Every year, 600 American women are shot to death by intimate partners [61] Of all women murdered with a gun in the US, half are killed by their intimate partners [61]
- Nearly 1 million women alive today report being shot or shot at by an intimate partner, [62] and 4.5 million women alive today report that an intimate partner threatened them with a gun [62]
- When an abuser has access to a gun, a domestic violence victim is five times more likely to be killed [63]
- Black women are twice as likely as white women to be fatally shot by an intimate partner [64]
- In 2019 alone, there were 984 children (under the age of 18) killed and 2,785 injured

In 1994, Congress passed an assault weapons ban that prohibited the sale of semi-automatic assault rifles and high-capacity magazines. That ban was in effect for a decade, but in 2004, it was allowed to lapse. It then became the responsibility of individual states to decide how to handle limits or bans on assault rifles. Neither Texas nor Ohio put any limits or bans in place.

Currently, only a handful of states have enacted assault weapon limits or bans: California, Connecticut, Hawaii, Maryland, Massachusetts, Minnesota, New Jersey, New York, Virginia, and Washington. Colorado has enacted a ban on large-capacity magazines.

Let's make one thing very clear: The only reason assault rifles exist is to kill a lot of people in a short amount of time. There is no other reason. No one needs to own this type of weapon for hunting or personal protection. No one.

And yet, so many people do, that these types of incidents aren't even front-page news anymore. They've become that commonplace. And that's not okay.

How Bad Is It?

We shouldn't have to ask this question as a country, but, unfortunately, we do. And even more unfortunately, the answer is simple. It's really, really bad. I highlighted the gun statistics for 2019 above, but let's take a look at 2018. That year, 337 mass shootings occurred, 24 at schools. More than 14,000 people were killed in gun incidents, and nearly 28,000 more were injured [65]. An estimated 290 million guns are owned in the United States, one for almost every man, woman, and child in the population.

School Shootings

First, let's all take a moment of silence to remember the worst school shootings in United States history. They are, in chronological order:

August 1, 1966
University of Texas, Austin, TX
Fatalities: **14**
Injuries: **31**

April 20, 1999
Columbine, Columbine, CO
Fatalities: **13**
Injuries: **24**

March 21, 2005
Red Lake High School, Red Lake, MN
Fatalities: **9**

<u>April 16, 2007</u>
Virginia Tech, Blacksburg, VA
    Fatalities: **32**
    Injuries: **17**

<u>December 14, 2012</u>
Sandy Hook Elementary School, Newtown CT
    Fatalities; **26**
    Injuries: **2**

<u>October 1, 2015</u>
Umpqua College, Roseburg, OR
    Fatalities: **10**
    Injuries: **7**

<u>February 14, 2018</u>
Marjory Stoneman Douglas HS, Parkland, FL
    Fatalities: **17**
    Injuries: **14**

Go back and read those numbers one more time. That's 121 young lives lost, for doing nothing more than pursuing an education. One-hundred-twenty-one families ripped apart for simply sending their children to what should be the safest place outside the home. Countless more were left traumatized, scared, and suffering.

I have three children, ages 18-24. When they were little, my biggest fear when they went off to school was that they might be picked on, or worse yet, bullied. I never feared for their lives, and the thought never, ever, occurred to me that they might not come back home due to a shooting.

No parent should have to fear that their child is not safe at school. It's time to stop the violence. And listen up: Bullet-proof backpacks are not the answer. Repeat that as necessary until it sinks in. I'll wait.

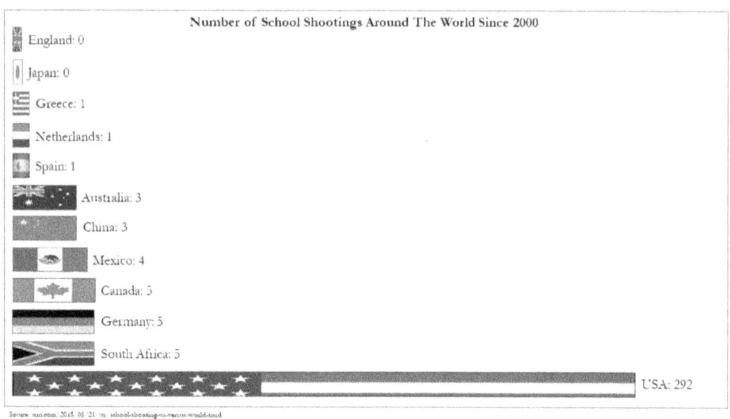

Other Mass Shootings

The Gun Violence Archive defines a "mass shooting" as an incident in which four or more people are shot. By that definition and according to the Archive, in America, there were 417 mass shootings in 2019, 337 in 2018, 346 in 2017; 382 in 2016; and 336 in 2015.

No other developed country sees anything close to these kinds of numbers, and it's not simply because more people live here. An attorney for the Law Center to Prevent Gun Violence attributes the United States' bloated gun violence numbers to the fact that the types of weapon most commonly used in these types of crimes are simply not available in other countries - weapons like the ones used in Las Vegas and Orlando, the two deadliest mass shootings in United States history.

Let's take a moment of silence to remember those incidents.

June 12, 2016
Pulse nightclub, Orlando FL
    Fatalities: **49**
    Injuries: **53**

October 1, 2017
Route 91 Harvest Music Fest, Las Vegas NV
    Fatalities: **59**
    Injuries: **422**

It's been 15 years since the federal ban on semiautomatic weapons was allowed to expire. In those years, the frequency and severity of United States mass shootings have only increased, and the weapons used most often are precisely the ones that had been subject to the prior ban.

Let's look at what the gunman in the Las Vegas shooting was equipped with: he had 24 firearms. Fourteen of them were AR-15 semi-automatic rifles, seven AR-10 type rifles, one bolt-action rifle, and one .38-caliber revolver. He also had a large quantity of ammunition, and numerous high-capacity magazines each capable of holding up to 100 rounds. The semi-automatic rifles were fitted with vertical forward grips and bump fire stocks (which allow for a firing rate of 90 rounds in 10 seconds). All the firearms and bump stocks were legally purchased. [66]

All of this of course begs the question: How long will we tolerate this in the United States? Because we are tolerating it. Our government is standing by, offering nothing more than thoughts and prayers, instead of taking action – any action – to prevent these heinous tragedies. That kind of inaction equals tolerating gun violence at best, and outright condoning it at worst.

To express the magnitude of the mass shootings in 2019 alone, listed here is each incident, the date it occurred, how many people were injured and how many killed, along with the location. Not all of you will take the 10 minutes required to read through this list in detail, but as you flip through the pages, let the statistics on this list sink in.

Why the Government is failing…"We the People"

Date	# Killed	# Injured	State	City Or County
29-Dec-19	0	5	Illinois	Danville
29-Dec-19	1	3	New York	Buffalo
29-Dec-19	0	5	California	Ceres
27-Dec-19	1	3	California	Modesto
27-Dec-19	0	4	Georgia	Kennesaw
27-Dec-19	2	7	Texas	Houston
26-Dec-19	0	5	Florida	Saint Petersburg
25-Dec-19	0	4	California	Oakland
25-Dec-19	1	3	Iowa	Coralville
25-Dec-19	1	3	Virginia	Richmond
24-Dec-19	0	4	Louisiana	New Orleans
24-Dec-19	0	6	North Carolina	High Point
22-Dec-19	0	7	Maryland	Baltimore
22-Dec-19	1	7	Minnesota	Minneapolis (Spring Lake Park)
22-Dec-19	0	13	Illinois	Chicago
21-Dec-19	1	6	Mississippi	Waynesboro
21-Dec-19	0	4	Louisiana	Edgard
20-Dec-19	2	2	Alabama	Tuskegee
18-Dec-19	0	4	Texas	San Antonio
17-Dec-19	4	1	Montana	Great Falls
15-Dec-19	1	4	Georgia	Columbus
14-Dec-19	0	4	California	Ivanhoe
12-Dec-19	1	3	Missouri	Saint Louis
10-Dec-19	6	3	New Jersey	Jersey City
8-Dec-19	2	3	Texas	Desoto
8-Dec-19	1	4	Louisiana	New Orleans
6-Dec-19	4	8	Florida	Pensacola
4-Dec-19	2	2	Alabama	Montgomery
1-Dec-19	2	3	Louisiana	Cotton Valley
1-Dec-19	2	2	Louisiana	New Orleans
1-Dec-19	1	4	Illinois	Aurora
1-Dec-19	1	3	Michigan	Kalamazoo
1-Dec-19	0	12	Louisiana	New Orleans
30-Nov-19	0	5	Arkansas	Hensley
29-Nov-19	0	7	Texas	Amarillo
27-Nov-19	0	5	New York	Bronx
25-Nov-19	2	2	Florida	Brownsville
24-Nov-19	1	4	Alabama	Birmingham
24-Nov-19	0	6	California	Los Angeles
24-Nov-19	2	2	Louisiana	Cottonport
23-Nov-19	1	6	Louisiana	Tallulah

Date			State	City
23-Nov-19	0	4	California	Los Angeles
21-Nov-19	0	5	California	Long Beach
21-Nov-19	0	4	Washington	Everett
20-Nov-19	0	4	California	Richmond
18-Nov-19	1	4	New Jersey	Newark
17-Nov-19	4	6	California	Fresno
17-Nov-19	0	4	Ohio	Cleveland
16-Nov-19	6	0	California	San Diego
14-Nov-19	3	3	California	Santa Clarita
11-Nov-19	0	4	Florida	Belle Glade
10-Nov-19	0	4	Missouri	Kansas City
10-Nov-19	1	4	Tennessee	Memphis
10-Nov-19	0	4	Arkansas	Little Rock
9-Nov-19	0	4	Michigan	Detroit
9-Nov-19	0	4	Georgia	Vidalia
8-Nov-19	1	3	North Carolina	Raleigh
7-Nov-19	2	3	Georgia	Conyers
4-Nov-19	1	4	Texas	Houston
3-Nov-19	0	4	Ohio	Toledo
3-Nov-19	1	3	Texas	Nacogdoches
2-Nov-19	0	4	Louisiana	Baton Rouge
2-Nov-19	1	4	Michigan	Detroit
1-Nov-19	0	5	Arizona	Tolleson
1-Nov-19	0	4	Texas	San Angelo
31-Oct-19	5	3	California	Orinda
30-Oct-19	4	0	Pennsylvania	Philadelphia
29-Oct-19	3	9	California	Long Beach
29-Oct-19	1	3	Maryland	Baltimore
28-Oct-19	1	3	Maryland	Baltimore
27-Oct-19	0	4	Michigan	Detroit
27-Oct-19	1	4	Michigan	Lansing
26-Oct-19	2	6	Texas	Greenville
24-Oct-19	2	2	Oklahoma	Oklahoma City
22-Oct-19	1	3	Oklahoma	Oklahoma City (Midwest City)
21-Oct-19	0	4	South Carolina	Sumter
20-Oct-19	1	3	Texas	Port Arthur
19-Oct-19	0	4	Pennsylvania	Duquesne
19-Oct-19	1	4	Texas	El Paso
15-Oct-19	0	4	Ohio	Columbus
13-Oct-19	0	6	Pennsylvania	Philadelphia
13-Oct-19	0	4	Ohio	Akron
12-Oct-19	4	3	New York	Brooklyn

Date			State	City
12-Oct-19	1	3	Pennsylvania	Philadelphia
12-Oct-19	5	0	Illinois	Chicago
12-Oct-19	1	3	Maryland	Baltimore
12-Oct-19	1	5	Michigan	Eastpointe
10-Oct-19	2	2	Florida	Tampa
10-Oct-19	0	5	Pennsylvania	Philadelphia
9-Oct-19	0	5	Massachusetts	Lowell
9-Oct-19	1	3	Maryland	Baltimore
7-Oct-19	5	0	Massachusetts	Abington
6-Oct-19	0	4	Colorado	Denver
6-Oct-19	4	5	Kansas	Kansas City
6-Oct-19	0	5	Indiana	Evansville
5-Oct-19	0	5	Missouri	Saint Louis
3-Oct-19	1	3	North Carolina	Roxboro
3-Oct-19	1	3	Missouri	Marshall
1-Oct-19	0	4	Missouri	Saint Louis
29-Sep-19	1	3	Illinois	Round Lake (Round Lake Park)
29-Sep-19	0	4	Wisconsin	Milwaukee
29-Sep-19	0	4	Florida	Jacksonville
29-Sep-19	0	4	Kansas	Claflin
29-Sep-19	4	0	Texas	Beaumont
24-Sep-19	1	3	Illinois	Chicago
23-Sep-19	2	2	Indiana	Gary
22-Sep-19	0	5	Missouri	Kansas City
21-Sep-19	0	4	Louisiana	New Orleans
21-Sep-19	2	8	South Carolina	Lancaster
21-Sep-19	0	6	Indiana	Indianapolis
21-Sep-19	4	0	Ohio	Cleveland
20-Sep-19	1	5	Louisiana	New Orleans
19-Sep-19	1	5	District of Columbia	Washington
18-Sep-19	3	1	Illinois	Chicago
18-Sep-19	2	2	California	Wilmington
16-Sep-19	2	2	Wyoming	Cheyenne
14-Sep-19	1	3	Missouri	Saint Louis
14-Sep-19	1	4	California	Oakland
14-Sep-19	0	4	Georgia	Lagrange
12-Sep-19	1	3	New Mexico	Albuquerque
12-Sep-19	4	2	New Mexico	Albuquerque
10-Sep-19	0	4	Illinois	Chicago
8-Sep-19	2	2	South Carolina	Sumter
8-Sep-19	1	3	Louisiana	Alexandria
7-Sep-19	3	1	North Carolina	Whiteville

Date			State	City
4-Sep-19	2	2	Louisiana	Marrero
4-Sep-19	0	4	Florida	Jacksonville
2-Sep-19	5	0	Alabama	Elkmont
2-Sep-19	2	2	North Carolina	Greensboro
2-Sep-19	0	4	Illinois	Chicago
1-Sep-19	1	3	Connecticut	Hartford
1-Sep-19	0	4	North Carolina	Rocky Mount
1-Sep-19	0	7	Alabama	Valley
1-Sep-19	0	4	Ohio	Toledo
31-Aug-19	8	23	Texas	Odessa
31-Aug-19	2	2	Pennsylvania	Philadelphia
31-Aug-19	1	3	North Carolina	Charlotte
31-Aug-19	0	4	South Carolina	Moncks Corner
31-Aug-19	0	4	Maryland	Baltimore
31-Aug-19	0	4	Maryland	Frederick
31-Aug-19	2	3	Illinois	Chicago
30-Aug-19	0	6	Alabama	Mobile
30-Aug-19	1	3	Maryland	Baltimore
29-Aug-19	1	3	Maryland	Baltimore
25-Aug-19	1	3	Illinois	Chicago
25-Aug-19	3	4	New Mexico	Hobbs
24-Aug-19	0	7	Maryland	Temple Hills (Camp Springs)
24-Aug-19	1	3	Massachusetts	Lynn
23-Aug-19	3	2	Texas	Houston
23-Aug-19	0	4	Georgia	Dublin
23-Aug-19	1	3	Missouri	Saint Louis
22-Aug-19	2	2	South Carolina	Columbia
22-Aug-19	0	4	California	Los Angeles
20-Aug-19	0	4	Georgia	Atlanta
18-Aug-19	0	4	Missouri	Kansas City
17-Aug-19	0	6	Texas	Houston
15-Aug-19	2	3	Alabama	Montgomery
15-Aug-19	0	5	Pennsylvania	Philadelphia
14-Aug-19	0	6	Pennsylvania	Philadelphia
13-Aug-19	2	3	Washington	Tacoma
12-Aug-19	0	4	Mississippi	Greenwood
11-Aug-19	0	6	Illinois	Chicago
10-Aug-19	0	4	Virginia	Richmond
10-Aug-19	0	4	California	San Francisco
9-Aug-19	0	4	Illinois	Chicago
7-Aug-19	3	1	Missouri	Saint Louis
5-Aug-19	0	4	New York	Brooklyn

4-Aug-19	0	4	Louisiana	Lake Charles
4-Aug-19	1	7	Illinois	Chicago
4-Aug-19	1	3	Tennessee	Memphis
4-Aug-19	0	7	Illinois	Chicago
4-Aug-19	10	17	Ohio	Dayton
3-Aug-19	22	24	Texas	El Paso
2-Aug-19	2	3	Virginia	Suffolk
30-Jul-19	0	5	Ohio	Columbus
28-Jul-19	4	17	California	Gilroy
28-Jul-19	1	5	Pennsylvania	Philadelphia
28-Jul-19	5	2	Wisconsin	Chippewa Falls
28-Jul-19	0	4	District of Columbia	Washington
28-Jul-19	0	4	Illinois	Chicago
27-Jul-19	1	3	Kansas	Wichita
27-Jul-19	1	11	New York	Brooklyn
26-Jul-19	1	3	Washington	Kennewick
25-Jul-19	4	2	California	Canoga Park
21-Jul-19	0	4	Illinois	Chicago
21-Jul-19	0	4	District of Columbia	Washington
20-Jul-19	0	4	Pennsylvania	Clairton
20-Jul-19	1	3	Maryland	Baltimore
20-Jul-19	0	7	Illinois	Chicago
18-Jul-19	1	3	Illinois	Chicago
17-Jul-19	1	3	Texas	Lubbock
16-Jul-19	0	4	Texas	San Antonio
15-Jul-19	0	4	Georgia	Atlanta
14-Jul-19	0	4	Illinois	Chicago
13-Jul-19	1	4	Illinois	Chicago
13-Jul-19	0	7	Pennsylvania	Philadelphia
11-Jul-19	0	4	Texas	Houston
8-Jul-19	2	2	District of Columbia	Washington
7-Jul-19	0	6	Michigan	Flint
7-Jul-19	0	5	Missouri	Saint Louis
7-Jul-19	0	4	Illinois	Chicago
7-Jul-19	0	4	Illinois	Chicago
7-Jul-19	0	4	New Mexico	Albuquerque
6-Jul-19	0	4	California	San Jose
6-Jul-19	5	0	Missouri	Saint Louis
5-Jul-19	0	6	Massachusetts	Boston
5-Jul-19	0	5	Illinois	Chicago
5-Jul-19	1	3	Nevada	Reno
5-Jul-19	0	4	New York	Brooklyn

4-Jul-19	0	4	Illinois	Rockford
4-Jul-19	1	3	Illinois	Chicago
4-Jul-19	0	4	California	Los Angeles
4-Jul-19	1	3	California	Fresno
3-Jul-19	2	3	Texas	Katy
2-Jul-19	0	4	Missouri	Saint Louis (Wellston)
1-Jul-19	0	4	Maryland	Baltimore
30-Jun-19	0	4	California	Oakland
30-Jun-19	0	5	California	Yucaipa
30-Jun-19	2	2	Texas	Dallas
30-Jun-19	0	6	New York	Bay Shore
29-Jun-19	0	4	Connecticut	Hartford
29-Jun-19	0	4	Louisiana	Gray
29-Jun-19	0	5	Illinois	Chicago
29-Jun-19	0	7	Louisiana	Baton Rouge
28-Jun-19	0	4	New Jersey	Paterson
28-Jun-19	0	5	Connecticut	Hamden
28-Jun-19	0	7	Georgia	Atlanta
28-Jun-19	0	4	New Jersey	Jersey City
28-Jun-19	0	5	Minnesota	Saint Paul
27-Jun-19	0	7	Georgia	Atlanta
26-Jun-19	1	3	Ohio	Akron
26-Jun-19	0	4	Wisconsin	Milwaukee
23-Jun-19	1	3	California	La Jolla
23-Jun-19	5	0	California	San Jose
23-Jun-19	1	10	Indiana	South Bend
23-Jun-19	0	5	Ohio	Columbus
23-Jun-19	3	1	South Carolina	Abbeville
22-Jun-19	0	4	Virginia	Hampton
22-Jun-19	0	4	Pennsylvania	Philadelphia
22-Jun-19	1	4	Maryland	Baltimore
21-Jun-19	1	3	Michigan	Saginaw
21-Jun-19	0	4	Illinois	Chicago
21-Jun-19	5	0	California	Santa Maria
21-Jun-19	0	5	California	Richmond
20-Jun-19	0	10	Pennsylvania	Allentown
18-Jun-19	1	4	New Jersey	Newark
17-Jun-19	0	4	Texas	San Antonio
17-Jun-19	0	5	Tennessee	Memphis
16-Jun-19	1	5	Pennsylvania	Philadelphia
16-Jun-19	1	6	Kentucky	Louisville
16-Jun-19	0	6	Iowa	Des Moines

15-Jun-19	0	4	Louisiana	Shreveport
12-Jun-19	1	3	North Carolina	Charlotte
11-Jun-19	0	4	Colorado	Aurora
11-Jun-19	2	2	Georgia	Savannah
9-Jun-19	1	3	Ohio	Cleveland
9-Jun-19	0	4	New York	Buffalo
9-Jun-19	1	3	Tennessee	Henning
8-Jun-19	5	2	Washington	White Swan
8-Jun-19	0	4	Illinois	Chicago
7-Jun-19	0	5	Texas	Austin
6-Jun-19	1	3	Illinois	Chicago
5-Jun-19	0	4	California	Santa Rosa
1-Jun-19	0	5	South Carolina	Allendale
1-Jun-19	0	4	Illinois	Chicago
1-Jun-19	1	3	Virginia	Portsmouth
1-Jun-19	0	4	Illinois	Chicago
1-Jun-19	0	5	Georgia	Atlanta
1-Jun-19	2	4	Georgia	Macon
31-May-19	13	4	Virginia	Virginia Beach
31-May-19	1	3	California	West Covina
30-May-19	0	5	Illinois	Robbins
29-May-19	3	2	Texas	Cleveland
29-May-19	1	3	Louisiana	Reserve
27-May-19	2	2	Missouri	Saint Louis
27-May-19	0	5	District of Columbia	Washington
27-May-19	1	5	New Jersey	Trenton
26-May-19	1	3	District of Columbia	Washington
26-May-19	0	5	Virginia	La Crosse
26-May-19	1	3	California	Stockton
25-May-19	0	9	New Jersey	Trenton
25-May-19	3	2	Michigan	Detroit
25-May-19	1	9	Virginia	Chesapeake
25-May-19	0	4	Maryland	Baltimore
25-May-19	0	5	Oklahoma	Oklahoma City
20-May-19	2	2	Oklahoma	Tulsa
20-May-19	1	4	Louisiana	Alexandria
20-May-19	0	4	Ohio	Columbus
19-May-19	0	5	Oregon	Portland
18-May-19	1	4	Mississippi	Cascilla
18-May-19	1	8	Alabama	Atmore
18-May-19	2	2	Iowa	Cedar Rapids
18-May-19	1	6	Indiana	Muncie

18-May-19	1	4	California	Long Beach
18-May-19	0	4	Nebraska	Omaha
18-May-19	2	4	North Carolina	Winston Salem (Winston-salem)
17-May-19	1	3	California	Sacramento
16-May-19	0	4	Ohio	Cleveland
15-May-19	0	4	Louisiana	Saint Rose
14-May-19	0	4	California	Los Angeles
13-May-19	0	4	Louisiana	New Orleans
13-May-19	4	1	Missouri	Saint Louis
11-May-19	0	4	Pennsylvania	Effort
10-May-19	0	5	Pennsylvania	Philadelphia
10-May-19	0	6	Missouri	Saint Louis
8-May-19	0	4	Indiana	Indianapolis
7-May-19	1	8	Colorado	Littleton (Highlands Ranch)
5-May-19	1	4	New Jersey	North Bergen
5-May-19	0	6	California	Oceano
4-May-19	1	4	Missouri	Saint Louis
4-May-19	0	4	Indiana	Indianapolis
4-May-19	1	4	California	Stockton
4-May-19	0	4	Delaware	Wilmington
3-May-19	1	3	Texas	Dallas
3-May-19	0	5	Maryland	Baltimore
3-May-19	0	4	Maryland	Baltimore
1-May-19	1	3	Massachusetts	Boston
30-Apr-19	2	4	North Carolina	Charlotte
28-Apr-19	0	7	Tennessee	Nashville
28-Apr-19	0	4	Alabama	Birmingham
28-Apr-19	1	7	Maryland	Baltimore
28-Apr-19	4	0	Ohio	West Chester
27-Apr-19	1	3	Mississippi	Jackson
27-Apr-19	1	3	California	Poway
27-Apr-19	0	6	California	Los Angeles
21-Apr-19	0	4	Pennsylvania	Philadelphia
20-Apr-19	0	5	Tennessee	Memphis
20-Apr-19	0	4	Texas	Corpus Christi
19-Apr-19	0	4	Kansas	Wichita
18-Apr-19	0	4	Kentucky	Louisville
16-Apr-19	1	3	Maryland	Germantown
14-Apr-19	0	4	California	Stockton
14-Apr-19	2	2	Florida	Miami
14-Apr-19	1	3	California	Vallejo
13-Apr-19	0	4	California	Moreno Valley

12-Apr-19	0	4	Illinois	Carbondale
11-Apr-19	1	3	Maryland	Baltimore
11-Apr-19	3	2	Arizona	Phoenix
11-Apr-19	1	4	California	Los Angeles
9-Apr-19	1	3	Missouri	Kansas City
7-Apr-19	2	2	Indiana	Indianapolis
7-Apr-19	0	7	North Carolina	Winston Salem (Winston-salem)
7-Apr-19	0	6	Delaware	Wilmington
7-Apr-19	0	4	Louisiana	Shreveport
6-Apr-19	0	4	Florida	Tallahassee
6-Apr-19	0	6	Illinois	Chicago
4-Apr-19	1	3	Florida	Panama City
4-Apr-19	3	2	Georgia	Stockbridge
2-Apr-19	0	4	Mississippi	Hermanville
2-Apr-19	0	5	Kentucky	Covington
31-Mar-19	1	4	Illinois	Chicago
31-Mar-19	1	4	Georgia	Atlanta
31-Mar-19	0	7	South Carolina	North Charleston
28-Mar-19	0	4	Maryland	Baltimore
25-Mar-19	0	5	Nevada	North Las Vegas
24-Mar-19	1	5	California	San Francisco
24-Mar-19	0	7	Arizona	Phoenix
19-Mar-19	2	4	Arizona	Phoenix
17-Mar-19	0	4	Georgia	Augusta
17-Mar-19	1	3	Georgia	Rochelle
17-Mar-19	0	4	Nevada	Las Vegas
16-Mar-19	1	3	New Jersey	Camden
15-Mar-19	2	4	Alabama	Mobile
14-Mar-19	1	3	Montana	Missoula
11-Mar-19	0	4	New Jersey	Paterson
10-Mar-19	0	4	Louisiana	Shreveport
10-Mar-19	1	4	Colorado	Denver
3-Mar-19	0	4	California	Oakland
3-Mar-19	0	6	Illinois	Chicago
2-Mar-19	1	4	Arkansas	Pine Bluff
28-Feb-19	1	3	California	Oakland
22-Feb-19	2	2	Alabama	Birmingham
21-Feb-19	1	4	Maryland	Baltimore
21-Feb-19	2	2	Kentucky	Elizabethtown
21-Feb-19	2	2	Texas	Houston
20-Feb-19	0	4	Tennessee	Covington
17-Feb-19	2	2	Texas	Henderson

Date			State	City
17-Feb-19	0	5	Indiana	Evansville
17-Feb-19	1	5	Louisiana	New Orleans
16-Feb-19	5	0	Mississippi	Clinton
15-Feb-19	6	6	Illinois	Aurora
11-Feb-19	5	0	Texas	Livingston
9-Feb-19	0	4	Virginia	Petersburg
6-Feb-19	1	3	New York	Brooklyn
5-Feb-19	2	2	Texas	San Antonio
4-Feb-19	0	5	District of Columbia	Washington
4-Feb-19	0	4	Louisiana	Baton Rouge
3-Feb-19	2	5	Illinois	Chicago
3-Feb-19	4	0	California	Palm Springs
1-Feb-19	0	4	California	San Diego
28-Jan-19	2	5	Texas	Houston
27-Jan-19	0	5	Alabama	Birmingham
26-Jan-19	0	4	Georgia	Albany
26-Jan-19	0	5	Indiana	Indianapolis
26-Jan-19	1	3	New Jersey	Newark
26-Jan-19	5	0	Louisiana	Gonzales
24-Jan-19	4	1	Pennsylvania	State College
24-Jan-19	4	1	Georgia	Rockmart
23-Jan-19	5	0	Florida	Sebring
20-Jan-19	0	4	Florida	Miami
19-Jan-19	0	4	Pennsylvania	Lebanon
19-Jan-19	1	4	South Carolina	Gaffney
19-Jan-19	0	4	Illinois	Chicago
19-Jan-19	3	2	Florida	Jacksonville
19-Jan-19	3	2	Texas	Houston
17-Jan-19	3	1	Kentucky	Owensboro
16-Jan-19	1	5	Florida	Jacksonville
16-Jan-19	3	1	California	Palmdale
15-Jan-19	1	4	Arkansas	Little Rock
13-Jan-19	1	5	Arizona	Phoenix
6-Jan-19	0	4	New Mexico	Roswell
4-Jan-19	3	2	Virginia	Hurt
4-Jan-19	3	4	California	Torrance
3-Jan-19	1	3	Arizona	Yuma
2-Jan-19	1	3	Arkansas	Jonesboro
1-Jan-19	0	5	South Carolina	Columbia
1-Jan-19	0	5	Florida	Tallahassee

State Gun Strength Rankings [67]

The Table on the right, lists each state in order of where they rank regarding Gun Death Rate per 100,000 people. The first column indicates where each state ranks regarding how weak or strong the gun laws are in that particular state (ranked weakest gun laws #1 to strongest gun laws #50)

If you look at the states with the highest death rate, you will see that they are also the states with the weakest gun laws (New Mexico is an outlier with a high death rate but fairly strong gun laws at #34). For example, Mississippi has the highest gun death rate and they also have the weakest gun laws. So, it ranks as #1 in both categories. Missouri and Wyoming follow a similar pattern. And so on.

Conversely, if you look at the 7 states with the lowest Gun Death Rate (California, Connecticut, New Jersey, New York, Hawaii, Massachusetts, and Rhode Island), it's no coincidence that they are all in the top 10 states with the strictest gun laws.

Gun Law Weakness (Ranked)	State	Gun Death Rate (Ranked)	Gun Death Rate (Per 100K)
1	Mississippi	1	22.81
13	Alabama	2	21.7
4	Missouri	3	21.34
18	Louisiana	4	21.31
2	Wyoming	5	21.09
34	New Mexico	6	20.75
9	Alaska	7	20.74
10	Arkansas	8	18.96
14	West Virginia	9	18.11
35	Nevada	10	17.84
22	Tennessee	11	17.82
20	South Carolina	12	17.51
15	Montana	13	17.27
5	Kentucky	14	16.81
11	Oklahoma	15	16.71
3	Idaho	16	16.61
19	Georgia	17	15.72
6	Arizona	18	15.29
37	Colorado	19	15.14
23	Indiana	20	14.71
8	Kansas	21	14.65
7	South Dakota	22	13.5
27	North Carolina	23	13.26
24	Utah	24	13.14
26	Ohio	25	13.05
31	Michigan	26	12.82
30	Florida	27	12.81
28	Vermont	28	12.63
39	Pennsylvania	29	12.47
16	Texas	30	12.22
25	Virginia	31	11.76
36	Oregon	32	11.68
45	Maryland	33	11.61
40	Delaware	34	11.55
12	North Dakota	35	11.36
43	Illinois	36	10.78
21	New Hampshire	37	10.66
41	Washington	38	10.32
17	Maine	39	10.32
29	Wisconsin	40	10.13
33	Nebraska	41	9.05
32	Iowa	42	8.62
38	Minnesota	43	7.79
50	California	44	7.45
48	Connecticut	45	4.91
49	New Jersey	46	4.75
47	New York	47	4.03
46	Hawaii	48	4.03
44	Massachusetts	49	3.46
42	Rhode Island	50	3.28

Domestic Violence

We must not ignore the fact that domestic violence and gun violence are angry, ugly siblings. On average, 52 women are killed each month by a domestic or intimate partner's gun. That's more than 600 women every year, year after year. Millions more have been shot at, wounded, or threatened by a domestic partner's gun. Women in the United States are 16 times more likely to be shot and killed than women in other developed countries. [68]

Domestic abusers have also wielded their weapons in mass attacks. Devin Kelley, the suspected attacker in a church shooting in Sutherland Springs, Texas, had been convicted in 2017 in a domestic violence incident, yet was somehow allowed to purchase an assault rifle. A person convicted in a domestic violence crime is prohibited under US law from possessing firearms, yet due to limited federal capacity to enforce these restrictions, this and all too many others somehow slipped through the cracks in one of many loopholes.

There are 47 percent fewer women shot to death by an intimate partner in states that require background checks on all handgun sales. [69]

According to the group, Everytown for Gun Safety, 54 percent of the mass shooters have committed domestic or family abuse. [70]

In 29 states, convicted stalkers can still legally buy and own guns. [70]

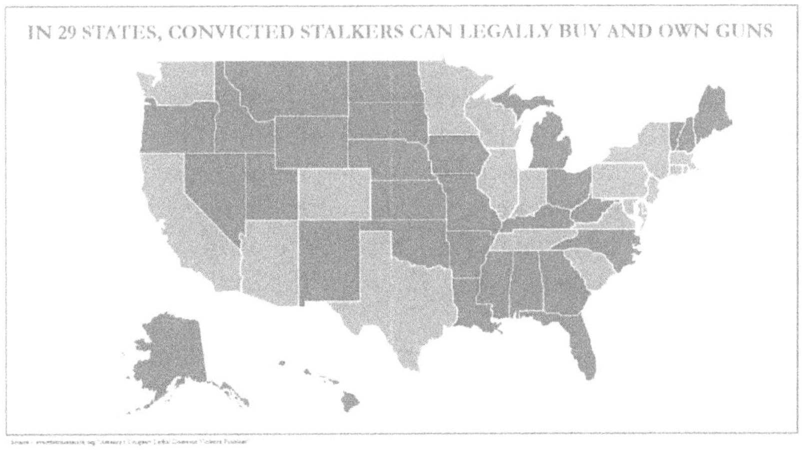

Suicide

Some argue against gun control or attempt to gloss over or downplay the severity of recent mass shootings, by pointing out that most of the gun fatalities in the United States are suicides, not random mass killings. That's true enough (about 60 percent of gun fatalities in this country are suicides), and heartbreaking. However, research indicates that most people who commit suicide do so very soon after making the decision. Guns make this far easier to accomplish, and those who attempt to commit suicide with a gun are much more likely to succeed than those who attempt it with other methods. While many people in this state of mind will, tragically, find another method if there's no gun available, there is some indication from other countries that this isn't always the case. The Israel Defense Forces stopped allowing troops to bring guns home on weekends, and suicide rates dropped by 40 percent, according to one study. Although not gun-related, the UK saw a drop in suicides after switching coal-gas stoves from a lethal-when-inhaled gas to an alternate fuel source. There was an increase in other methods of suicide, but suicides overall decreased.

My point here is that reducing the availability of guns will save lives, whether those lives would have been lost to suicides or mass rampages. They're both heinous.

Let's Talk Mental Health

A common thread that runs through many shootings, whether a mass shooting, a domestic violence attack, or a suicide, is the mental health of the person with the gun. While there are laws to prevent those suffering from mental illnesses to purchase guns, they are often ineffective. Background checks are sporadic and often not enforced. In some places, if the background report isn't back within 72 hours, the applicant can go ahead and buy the gun.

Health Insurance Portability and Accountability Act (HIPAA) rules do allow mental health providers to share the identities of patients with a mental health issue that would prevent them from possessing a firearm, but enforcement after the fact is overlooked. What if the person already owns a gun, and subsequently begins treatment for a mental health issue? Gun ownership should be checked at the start of treatment and the gun(s) confiscated and the license revoked.

WTF Are We Doing?

In response to the Marjory Stoneman Douglas High School shooting in Florida, the following week President Trump tweeted "If a potential 'sicko shooter' knows that a school has a large number of very weapons talented teachers (and others) who will be instantly shooting, the sicko will NEVER attack that school. Cowards won't go there…problem solved."

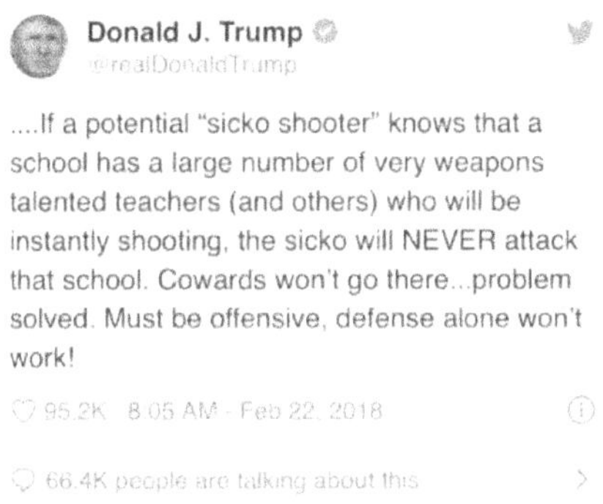

It appears at least 95 thousand people agreed with him. I, for one, don't think arming teachers in the classroom is the solution to the problem. What if one of the teachers we are arming has mental issues and decides to start shooting our children?

The NRA has a slogan that says "the only thing that stops a bad guy with a gun is a good guy with a gun". A National Bureau of Economic Research study, co-authored by Stanford University law professor John Donohue, looked at gun violence as it coincides with concealed carry, or right to carry laws. The study found that the "good guy with the gun" was not a viable solution to gun violence. In fact, Donohue told ABC News that concealed carry laws seemed to increase violent crime, not reduce or deter it. [76].

Here are some other solutions being proposed:

Following the Sandy Hook Elementary School shooting in 2012, Guard Dog Security started selling bulletproof backpacks. The backpacks will protect against a 9mm and .44 magnum weapons but will not fully protect a student from an assault rifle, like the one used in the Marjory Stoneman Douglas High School shooting. According to a company spokesperson, there is a noticeable increase in sales after each mass shooting. That fact is alarming! Once again, I'm not sure bulletproofing our children is the answer to gun violence at schools.

A school district in Charleston County, South Carolina, has installed three armored, bulletproof doors as part of a pilot program. Really? I think we are dancing around the true issue here. Bulletproof doors and backpacks are not the answer. Next, we will be offering children defense courses on how not to get shot at school.

So, what can we do to stop the madness? I believe the US could go a long way in stopping the violence by focusing on several initiatives. First, closing the loopholes that allow guns to land where they shouldn't, including enacting and enforcing strict and thorough background checks. Second, increasing penalties for gun-related crimes to mandatory life sentences without parole. Third, learning from what other countries have successfully done to curb gun violence. And fourth, taking away the immense power of wealthy gun lobbyists – specifically the NRA – so laws can actually start changing.

Close the Loopholes

We must make buying a gun more difficult. Under current laws and the current state of enforcing what laws do exist, it is far, far too easy to buy a gun, and there are far, far too many loopholes that make it even easier.

Background checks must be tightened up and made non-negotiable. Dylann Roof, who killed nine people at a church in Charleston, South Carolina on June 17, 2015, should have been barred from purchasing a gun due to a prior drug possession charge. During the background check, the examiner failed to obtain the police report from the drug incident, and he was allowed to buy the gun.

When 14 people were killed at a holiday party in San Bernardino, California by a husband and wife, four guns were recovered from the attackers, including two assault rifles that had been bought by the perpetrators' neighbor. All four guns were obtained legally under California laws.

Before Aaron Alexis killed 12 people at the Washington Navy Yard on September 16, 2013, he had sought treatment from the VA for psychiatric issues. He was (thankfully) stopped from purchasing an assault rifle but passed all background checks in Virginia to buy the shotgun he used in the attack.

On July 23, 2015, at a movie theater in Lafayette, Louisiana, John R. Houser killed 2 people and wounded 9 others using a .40-caliber semiautomatic pistol which he purchased from a pawnshop. In 2006, Houser was accused of domestic violence and soliciting arson. In 2008, a judge ordered him sent to a psychiatric hospital. He was still able to purchase his weapon legally in 2014 even though he had been denied a concealed weapon permit earlier.

On January 8, 2011, Jared L. Loughner killed six people with a Glock handgun in a supermarket parking lot in Tucson, Arizona. In 2007 Loughner was arrested for possession of drug paraphernalia. The following year he failed a drug test when trying to enlist in the Army. In 2010, he was forced to withdraw from community college because of campus officials' fears about the safety of the staff and students. Yet none of this prior history stopped Loughner from purchasing a gun in November 2010.

On July 20, 2012, James E. Holmes, who killed 12 and wounded 70 at a Colorado movie theater, was currently in treatment with a psychiatrist, yet was legally allowed to buy four guns in the weeks leading up to the shooting.

On April 2, 2014, Specialist Ivan Antonio Lopez opened fire at Fort Hood with a semiautomatic pistol, killing three people and wounding 16 others. As recently as a month prior to the shooting, Lopez had been seen by a military psychiatrist and was being treated for depression and anxiety. Oddly enough, he bought his gun at the same shop where Nidel Malik Hasan had bought one of his guns used in the 2009 mass shooting, also at Fort Hood, that killed 13 people.

One of the saddest mass shootings in history, occurred on December 14, 2012, at the Sandy Hook Elementary School in Newtown Connecticut. Adam Lanza, 20, first shot and killed his mother in their home, then went on to kill 26 people, mostly young children. Years before the shooting, Adam was diagnosed with psychiatric and physical ailments like anxiety and obsessive-compulsive disorder, which were never treated. He used his mother's guns to kill her and the 26 others.

I could go on, but it gets as repetitive as it is horrifying. It bears repeating that it is simply too easy to buy a gun in our country. This must change.

The National Instant Criminal Background Check System (NICS) is a background check that is governed at the federal level. This check is only required when the seller is a federally registered gun dealer. Most checks are performed relatively quickly, usually within minutes. If the check cannot be determined within 3 business days, the gun sale can be completed. There are also major concerns with the incomplete and poorly maintained NICS data.

Nineteen states and Washington, D.C. do require background checks on all handgun sales, but all other states only require the checks at licensed gun dealers. That means gun shows, trade shows, and private sales are not subject to these requirements. We must close this loophole. Oh, and those states that do require background checks on all sales? They see 47 percent fewer domestic violence gun deaths than states that don't.

Conflicting federal and state laws create further loopholes that allow guns to get into hands they shouldn't fall into. These need to be closed.

Those who enter treatment for mental health concerns must surrender their guns.

Federal and state laws need to be increased and aligned, and government entities must do better at working together to prevent violence.

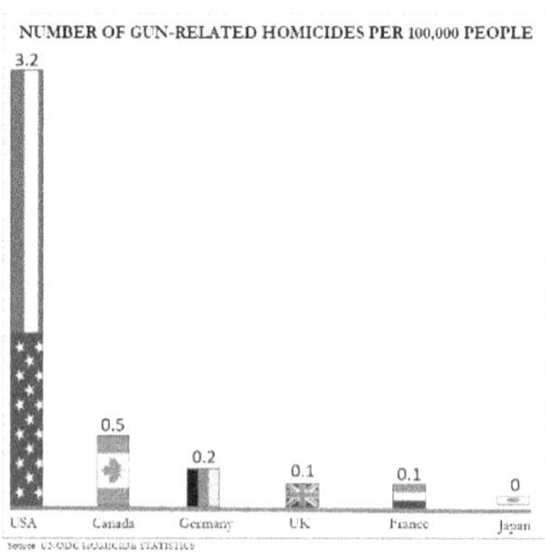

What Can We Learn from Other Countries?

Why aren't we changing the laws? Germany, Australia, the UK, and New Zealand have all experienced shootings that caused them to turn around and make their gun laws stricter. Why aren't we doing this in the United States?

New Zealand

Let's look at New Zealand. Prior to the March 2019 shooting in a mosque that left 50 people dead, the country had not endured a mass shooting in almost 30 years. The government's reaction was swift and sweeping – a nation-wide ban on assault weapons was announced within a week.

After the Las Vegas shooting, it took the United States more than a year to ban the bump stocks which the killer used to convert semi-automatic weapons to fully automatic.

Singapore

Although I'm not advocating that we go so far as Singapore's gun laws, which disallow anyone from owning a gun and beat by caning anyone caught with one, along with a mandatory death sentence if a firearm is used in a crime regardless of fatality or injury, we do need to follow some other global examples.

Australia

When 35 people were killed and 23 injured in a mass shooting in Australia in 1996, the government restricted ownership of pump-action shotguns and high-capacity semi-automatic rifles. Approximately 650,000 Australians turned in assault weapons under a buy-back program.

Great Britain

In Great Britain, after a mass shooting in 1987 (semi-automatic weapons were immediately banned and the laws were made even stricter in 1996), only the police, military, and certain people with written permission from the home office secretary are allowed to own guns. That written permission isn't handed out easily, either. Self-defense is not included in "good reasons" to own guns, and hunters wanting to practice their sport on their own property have been denied.

Germany

Germany, who already had solid gun rules in place, made it even more difficult to buy guns after a school shooting in 2003. Laws were revised once again after 15 people were killed in a school shooting in 2009.

And yet, since the Sandy Hook massacre of elementary-aged school children in 2012, the United States federal government has done....pretty much nothing.

Canada

Prior to April 18, 2020, Canadian laws divided guns into three categories: non-restricted, restricted, and prohibited. Semi-automatic weapons were considered restricted, requiring detailed background information and a waiting period of 28 days. Automatic weapons were prohibited.

On April 18, 2020 (during the writing of this chapter) Gabriel Wortman, 51, shot 13 people in Novia Scotia. Wortman was carrying several semi-automatic handguns and at least two semi-automatic rifles, one of which was described as a military-style assault weapon. Only one of the weapons could be traced back to Canada. Police believe the gunman acquired some of his weapons from the United States.

As a result of this, the worst ever mass murder in Canada, Prime Minister Justin Trudeau announced the ban of assault-style weapons. Trudeau said at a news conference in Ottawa: *"So, effective immediately, it is no longer permitted to buy, sell, transport, import or use military-grade assault weapons in this country." Trudeau went on to say, "These weapons were designed for one purpose, and one purpose only, to kill the largest number of people in the shortest amount of time. There is no use and no place for such weapons in Canada".* [71]

Japan

Japan's gun laws are perhaps the oldest on the books, dating back to the mid-16th century. Although it's legal to own several types of firearms, extensive instruction, tests, and background information is required. Applicants are also required to pass a mental health exam. Guns must be available for annual inspection, a practice that could help the United States close the mental-health-treatment-after-purchase loophole.

So, Does Gun Control Work?

The research and statistics say yes. A 2015 study by University of Alabama professor Adam Lankford found that adjusted for population, Yemen is the only country that suffers a higher rate of mass shootings than we do in the United States. Yemen is second behind the United States in the gun-ownership rate. Professor Lankford's study indicated that a country's rate of gun ownership correlated with the likelihood of a mass shooting, a correlation that held even when he removed the United States from the equation.

Less gun ownership isn't just tied to fewer mass shootings, either. A study out of the University of Berkeley found that the United States isn't more crime-ridden than other developed countries. But we are more prone to deadly crimes. In other words, a citizen in another country is just as likely to be robbed as an American. Here, however, it's more likely to result in a gun murder – about 54 times more likely in fact.

Gun control reform is a classic example of where I blame the government for failing us. Instead of doing what is right and just, politicians are too hung up fighting to hold to their party line.

Danielle Kurtzleben published on NPR the following list of bills that have been enacted into law or have failed to be enacted. As you can see, most have failed. What you may not know is that the reason some gun laws fail is that gun control votes tend to fall sharply along party lines.

Democrats, who favor gun control more than Republicans, tend to be more likely than Republicans to break ranks. [72]

- ***Brady Bill (1993, House and Senate):*** *Enacted into law. Refers to the Brady Handgun Violence Prevention Act. Passed in 1993, the Brady bill established five-day waiting periods and required background checks for gun purchases.*
- ***Assault Weapons Ban (1994, House and Senate):*** *Enacted into law, <u>expired in 2004</u>. This law banned people from making, selling or owning certain types of semiautomatic weapons.*
- ***Closing Gun Show Loophole (1999, House and Senate):*** *Did not become law. This refers to separate measures in each chamber that would have (broadly speaking) required people purchasing guns at gun shows to undergo a background check and a three-day waiting period.*
- ***Protection of Lawful Commerce in Arms Act (2005, House and Senate):*** *Enacted into law. This measure <u>protects firearm manufacturers</u> from being sued for crimes committed with the firearms they manufactured.*
- ***Concealed Carry Reciprocity (2011 and 2017, House; 2013, Senate):*** *Did not become law. These bills would have allowed a person with a concealed-carry permit in one state to legally carry a concealed firearm in other states.*
- ***Manchin-Toomey Bill (2015, Senate):*** *Did not become law. This bill would have required background checks for the purchase of guns at gun shows and online.*
- ***Murphy Amendment (2016, Senate):*** *Did not become law. This measure would have expanded background checks to cover guns sold online and at gun shows.*
- ***Feinstein Amendment (2016, Senate):*** *Did not become law. This measure would have barred people on terrorist watch lists from buying firearms.*
- ***Mental Health (2017, House and Senate):*** *Enacted into law. This bill <u>undid</u> an Obama-era regulation that added some people with mental illnesses to the FBI's background check database.*

Lobbying - The NRA

The following article, <u>When Lobbying was Illegal</u>, was written by Alex Mayyasi, for Priceonomics.

Wouldn't it be nice if lobbying were illegal? It's a tempting thought. But it seems impossible. Lobbying is a multi-billion dollar industry and an accepted—if hated—part of American politics. American courts have ruled that lobbying is constitutionally protected free speech, and lawyers and laymen alike generally accept this.

The same is true of more indirect lobbying, like the Citizens United Supreme Court ruling that allows businesses to spend unlimited sums of money on Super Pacs and advertisements for or against a candidate.

Yet from America's founding through much of the 19th century, the legal system treated lobbying as a corrupt and illegitimate activity. Lobbying still happened, but a number of states made lobbying a criminal offense, and the federal government banned some forms of lobbying. This all happened without legal challenge, as the courts viewed lobbying as incompatible with the rights and responsibilities of citizenship.

This forgotten history of lobbying in America has been documented by Zephyr Teachout, an Elizabeth Warren-style academic turned activist-politician who believes that Americans—and American legal minds—have forgotten the long American tradition of treating lobbying as a violation of a citizen's responsibility to represent only him or herself in the political process.

So how did we go from treating lobbying as illegitimate or illegal to protected free speech?

In 1785, the King of France gave Benjamin Franklin a diamond-encrusted snuffbox.

The gift was not a comment on Franklin's rumored inclination toward drug use. It was a customary parting gift. Franklin had represented America as a diplomat in France, and in royal Europe, a rich gift was a sign of respect.

In the uncouth, young nation of America, though, the gift was seen as dangerous. According to the Articles of Confederation, Congress had to approve any gift from a foreign official.

"At the level of basic human intercourse, Franklin owed something to the king after receiving such a gift," Zephyr Teachout writes. "These subtle sympathies threatened to corrupt Franklin because they could interfere with his responsibility to put the country's interest first in his diplomatic judgments."

Teachout opens her book Corruption in America with this incident in order to show how differently early Americans treated lobbying. And the contrast is stunning.

Over the past two decades, the Supreme Court has sanctioned any lobbying that is not explicit, quid pro quo bribery.

A 1999 Supreme Court case, for example, overturned a federal law that banned officials from receiving gifts. A farmer's association had given the Secretary of Agriculture sports tickets, luggage, and free meals—all delivered by hiring the Secretary's college roommate as a lobbyist—and then benefited from policies made by the Secretary. Yet the court sanctioned the act. Justice Scalia wrote that banning all gifts would lead to "absurdities," and he could not imagine banning an organization from organizing a free lunch for a policymaker.

…This logic and these conclusions, Teachout contends, are a complete break from the reasoning of judges in 18th and 19th century America.

For 100 years, judges so believed that using personal influence to ingratiate and gain access to lawmakers led to corruption that they refused to enforce lobbying contracts. Teachout cites a 19th century legal textbook that stated that "what are known as 'lobbying contracts'. . . [which are] any agreements to render services in procuring legislative action… by personal solicitation of the legislators or other objectionable means, is contrary to the plainest principles of public policy, and is void." For decades, when businesses failed to pay lobbyists, America's courts considered their employment unlawful and refused to make the businesses pay their lobbyists' fees.

Judges also did not object when legislators banned lobbying. In 1877, Georgian legislators wrote "Lobbying is declared to be a crime" into the state constitution. A number of state legislatures took similar action—for a time, lobbying was a felony in California—and in 1852, Congress passed a law banning anyone "employed as an agent to prosecute any claim pending before Congress" from being present during legislative sessions.

In 1999, Scalia considered it absurd that lawmakers should not be allowed to accept any gifts—he pointed out that this meant the president could not accept a jersey from the Patriots if they won the Super Bowl. But early Americans considered the dangers of gift-giving so alarming that they endured those absurdities—like forcing Benjamin Franklin, a retiring diplomat, to ask Congress to vote on whether he could keep his parting gift from the leader of France.

...So, what changed?

The First Amendment—and the perceived right to lobby—is not the only Constitutional Amendment whose meaning has changed dramatically over time.

Although it seems like established canon today that the Second Amendment guarantees the right to own a gun, this idea is a recent development. As recently as 1990, the conservative former Chief Justice Warren Burger denounced the idea that the Second Amendment offers an "unfettered individual right to a gun" as a "fraud on the American public." Describing the Second Amendment as a "gun control amendment," New Yorker writer Adam Gopnik writes that legal thought had long focused on the phrase "well regulated" in "a well regulated Militia."

Journalists and historians chronicling the recent change in the interpretation of the Second Amendment seem to agree on the story: The National Rifle Association and like-minded allies funded and cultivated a revisionist movement in legal thought that found its triumphant expression in 2008, when Justice Scalia struck down Washington D.C.'s ban on handguns.

This was the first articulation of this logic; previously, as Justice John Paul Stevens wrote, the amendment was always understood as allowing the regulation of the private use of firearms—as long as it didn't interfere with the upkeep of a regulated militia.

According to Teachout, our understanding of lobbying and the First Amendment underwent a similar, if longer and less consciously orchestrated, revisionary process. One of the first blows came in 1890, when Massachusetts passed a law requiring that lobbyists register with the government. Several states followed, which gave the sense that lobbyists were accepted professionals, rather than rogues improperly selling their personal influence.

A second development was the court's increasing inclination to honor and protect all contracts. In the past, courts had given more consideration to whether the contracts served public interests, which was the justification for refusing to enforce lobbying contracts.

The idea that lobbying was a legitimate enterprise and protected by the First Amendment slowly gained a legal foundation. Yet it's striking that as late as 1941, the Supreme Court debated and ruled on a case involving lobbying without invoking the First Amendment and free speech.

…Even as judges condemned lobbying with fire and brimstone rhetoric, the term 'lobbying' gained prominence in the early 1800s as railroad companies sought contracts and land from legislators. But lobbyists often did not need to ingratiate and subtly influence; they simply bribed outright.

The letters of the railroad baron Leland Stanford, who later served as governor and senator of California, are full of embarrassingly frank details about bribes, kickbacks, and monopolies. During the golden age of vote buying in New York, Tammany Hall politician George W. Plunkitt famously explained the difference between "honest and dishonest graft." In 1877, when the Georgia legislature banned lobbying, they did so after it came to light that lawmakers had sold 35 million acres of land to a business conglomerate for a scandalously low price. All but one of the lawmakers had been given shares in the business venture.

When Georgians discovered the scale of the corrupt land sale, they literally set fire to the documents used by the government to grant the land in a giant bonfire presided over by the Speaker of the House and President of the Senate. It was like they were ceremoniously burning the possessions of a boyfriend or girlfriend who had scorned them.

It's hard to say whether America has become more or less corrupt since then. Researchers who study the topic note that most hard data comes from subjective surveys, which are recently initiated and simply ask people about their perceptions of corruption. America does fairly well in these surveys, ranking 16th in the world as of 2015. But explicit bribery still *exists: Between 1990 and 2002, 10,000 officials were convicted for corrupt acts.*

The corruption that dominates headlines today, however, is mostly the legal kind: Bank regulators who act feckless so they can move onto plush banking jobs; Super Pacs that receive millions of dollars from companies that want access and influence; and lobbyists who take out lawmakers for expensive lunches.

The result is the cynical political culture that 19th-century judges worried about when they refused to sanction even lobbying that seemed above board. Nearly half of all members of Congress now take lobbying jobs when they leave office. Congressmen have written that serving on a congressional committee is now "mainly valuable as part of the interview process for a far more lucrative job as a K Street lobbyist" and that it has "become routine to see members of Congress drop their seat in Congress like a hot rock when a particularly lush vacancy opens up."

Since 2014, as journalist Ezra Klein points out, businesses have spent more money lobbying Congress than taxpayers have spent funding Congress.

We have traded an era in which bribery was widespread but provoked outrage and consequences when it was discovered for an age in which corruption is condemned but seen as inevitable, legal, and even constitutional" [73]

No government official in any political party is willing to go up against the NRA. That's how powerful the organization is. Bribery and lobbying are a form of political corruption, with none more powerful than the NRA, and this must be stopped.

The NRA loves to say they're protecting your Second Amendment right to bear arms. Setting aside for a moment the fact that they're only interested in protecting their own political power, let me point something out: When the Second Amendment was written, the right to bear arms referred to militias with muskets, not unchecked civilians with assault rifles. I'm not saying you can't own a gun for protection or hunting. But no one needs an assault rifle.

Now that we've established that, let's get back to the corruption perpetuated and perpetrated by the NRA.

According to many polls over the years, most American citizens say they're in favor of stricter gun laws in some capacity. But officials elected by these citizens fail over and over to make that happen. Why?

The NRA.

Let's take a look at some of the largest NRA recipients (2017):

- John McCain, AZ, $7.7M
- Richard Burr, NC, $6.9M
- Roy Blunt, MO, $4.5M
- Thom Tillis, NC, $4.4M
- Cory Gardner, CO, $3.8M
- Marco Rubio, FL, $3.3M
- Joni Ernst, IA, $3.1M
- Rob Portman, OH, $3M
- Todd Young, IN, $2.8M
- Bill Cassidy, LA, $2.8M

All Republicans, each politician listed above offered thoughts, prayers, and support after the largest mass shooting in United States history in Las Vegas. None took any action. If that is not a failure of We, the People, by our government, then I don't know what is.

Much of the NRA's spending is funneled through political ads, both in favor of their chosen candidates or against their opponents. Relatively little of its spending goes directly to any one candidate, a tactic that has proven successful at both electing their chosen candidates and defeating their opponents – and in flying under the radar when it comes to political campaign contributions.

Ted Strickland, an Ohio Democrat who had secured the NRA's endorsement, found himself the subject of a large ad campaign against him after he backed a ban on assault weapons.

What makes the NRA so difficult to go up against is two-fold: the organization has very deep pockets (dues from its five million members and large contributions from the likes of Smith & Wesson and political group

Freedom Partners add up to very large amounts of money), and a large and loyal grassroots following.

Lobbying must be made illegal. The practice of buying elections and cloaking it in words like "advertising" and "lobbying" doesn't mean this isn't corruption in its purest form. It is. And if anything is going to change, the lobbyists have to go.

I'll leave this chapter with a bit of irony…

On June 25, 2019, there was an article posted by Hope Schrieber on Yahoo Lifestyle reporting that a Ford car dealer in Alabama was giving away a free bible, an American Flag, and a 12-gauge shotgun to anyone who purchased a car. [74]

Literally the next day on June 26, a gunman in Morgan Hill, California, who had recently been fired, shot and killed two people at a Ford car dealer. [75]

I am not trying to take away your constitutional right to own a gun. What I am trying to do is stop guns from ending up in the wrong hands. I am also saying that assault rifles and high capacity magazines don't have a place in our society.

In other words, Let's stop the madness!

Charity - National Compassion Fund

*"The National Compassion Fund provides a single, trusted way for the public to donate **directly** to victims of a mass crime, such as a shooting or terrorist attack. It has been developed by the National Center for Victims of Crime in partnership with victims and family members from past mass casualty crimes, including those from Sandy Hook, Aurora, Virginia Tech, Oak Creek Temple, NIU, Columbine, and 9/11.*

The National Compassion Fund (The Fund) serves donors by honoring their intent and crime victims by distributing donations directly to them."

Website - nationalcompassionfund.org/about

"Money is only a tool. It will take you wherever you wish, but it will not replace you as the driver."
- **Ayn Rand**

"Never spend your money before you have it."
-**Thomas Jefferson**

I'll start this chapter with a big ole number (or two): Our national deficit is expected to pass $1 trillion in 2020. That's trillion, with a "T". That's a pretty big shortfall, folks. And that's not to be confused with our current national debt, which sits as of March 2020 at $23.5 trillion. According to US Economy and News, "A budget **deficit** occurs when a country, business, or an individual has spending that is greater than the revenue they receive over a specific period—usually measured as a year. ... On a government-level, the national **debt** is the accumulation of each year's deficit.". As of June 2020, due to the multiple Coronavirus Aid, Relief, and Economic Security Acts (CARES), the budget deficit has hit an all-time high at $864 Billion.

When did our spending as a country spiral this far out of control? It happed slowly, and the area where most of that spending happens might surprise you. In his piece titled "Why America is Going Broke," John F. Cogan, author and the Leonard and Shirley Ely Senior Fellow at Stanford University's Hoover Institution, breaks down the major categories of national spending since 1947. He points out that, since the end of World War II, federal tax revenue has grown 15 percent faster than national income, while federal spending has ballooned at a rate of 50 percent faster. The main culprit? Entitlements, including Social Security, Medicare, Medicaid, food-stamps, and other welfare programs.

All told, about two-thirds of federal spending goes to entitlements. Defense spending and wars, while costly, only come in at one-sixth of federal spending today. Even in the times of Vietnam, Iraq, and Afghanistan and other wars, any increase in federal defense spending failed to touch the rapid growth of entitlement funding. Now that the baby boomers are collecting their government payouts from Social Security and Medicare in larger and larger numbers, well, the problem isn't exactly going to resolve itself. Either taxes or debt - or both - will continue to rise. [77]

I want you to take a guess as to when the US started accumulating debt. Think it over for a few minutes. Make a mental note of your guess.

The answer is farther back than many of you probably thought. The national debt is actually older than the country itself. That's right. After the colonies signed the Articles of Confederation and started the move toward independence from England, the leaders of this fledgling nation immediately started borrowing money. (Perhaps it's not surprising that debt of all sorts is such a common fact of life for most Americans. It's practically in our DNA.) We came out of the American Revolutionary War with a national debt of $75 million. That was in the 1780s, folks. After this and other early wars in our nation's history, the government did pay down some of the accumulated debt. But that practice is long gone.

Let's take a step back for a minute and look closer at the history of our national debt. Matt Phillips published an article in The Atlantic, titled <u>The Long Story of US Debt, From 1790 to 2011, in 1 Little Chart</u>. [78]

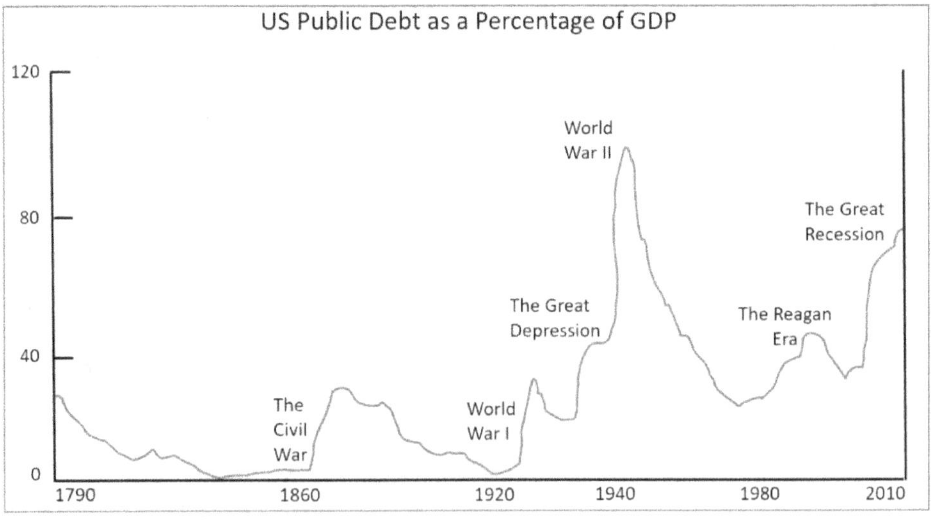

We can look to the 1930s, during the depths of the Great Depression, to see when our national spending started to skyrocket and debt became something to ignore rather than try to get out of. The government pumped all the money it could beg and borrow into boosting the stagnant economy, with no thought about how - or whether - to pay that debt down at some future point. Our complacency with an ever-growing national debt was thus born. The arguments about government spending and economic growth that still rage today were also born during this time.

Although we have established that defense is not this country's biggest spending category, the fact remains that wars are costly and pack a huge economic wallop. Let's take a look at wars and debt.

The Civil War

Prior to the Civil War, the country's debt was low. As you might expect, fighting a years-long war with yourself comes with a hefty price tag. By 1866, the country was in the hole to the tune of nearly $3 billion. Although growth in the decades that followed, combined with inflation, reduced the debt as a percentage of the country's economy, it wouldn't fall below about $900 million.

The Great War (aka World War I)

Heading into what was then known as the Great War, debt occupied less than 3 percent of the US economy. The government sold bonds to the public to pay for our entrance and participation in the conflict, and by the time the war ended, that 3 percent had grown to 33 percent. In actual numbers, the debt post-World War I sat at $25 billion, or around $335 billion in today's dollars. Just as during the years after the Civil War, measures were taken at this time to reduce that debt, which the country did, by about a third.

World War II

The post-Great Depression conflict that was World War II pushed the country's debt-to-GDP ratio to an eye-popping high of 113 percent. Although the national mindset had shifted and the government never really put any effort into paying that down (debt totaled $242 billion, or $2.9 trillion today), the debt proportion shrank as the US economy grew in the 1950s and '60s. The most recent low came in 1974 when debt sat at about 24 percent.

Reaganomics, 9/11 and the Great Recession

Moving away from wars, let's visit the 1980s for a minute. Remember that term? Reaganomics? Early in President Reagan's first term, the country fell into a recession spurred by high-interest rates aimed at curbing inflation. The country responded by increasing its spending on defense and those pesky entitlement programs that eat up so much of our budget. This marked one of the only times the country's national deficit surged outside of wartime.

By the mid-1990s however, the first President Bush had enacted his infamous tax increases ("Read my lips..." anyone?), followed by more tax increases during the Clinton administration, and the debt load became more manageable.

When Bush-the-second took office and on into the early 2000s, things looked so stable that there was actually some rumbling about paying off the national debt over the next 10 years. Needless to say, it didn't work out that way. Spending increased again after the 9/11 terrorist attacks, and the country was also hurtling at breakneck speed toward the cliff that was the banking and housing crisis.

Which brings us to the Great Recession of 2008 and '09 (although we may be headed for a worse recession now, as a result of the Covid-19 shutdown). At this point, the debt-to-GDP ratio took a double whammy as consumer and business spending plummeted and government spending climbed.

First, some numbers: In 2018, the US imported $539.5 billion dollars' worth of goods from China - a record. That same year, we exported just

$120.3 billion in goods to China, according to Jeffry Bartash and his piece <u>Why the US/China Trade Deficit is so Huge: Here's all the Stuff America Imports</u>.

At the top of the list of imported goods, we find computers, electronics, and electrical equipment (including that cell phone you can't stop checking), coming in at a combined $236.4 billion. Machinery, clothes, metal, furniture, transportation equipment, chemicals, and general manufactured products of plastic, rubber, and leather are also among the mountain of imports from China to the US. That's a lot.

Disputes about fair trade practices in recent years haven't gotten far, and President Trump has raised tariffs on nearly every imported product as a result, meaning American families could be paying more (although so far the tariffs have hit China worse than they have America). [79]

This long-standing and growing imbalance between the two countries has resulted in many products ceasing any domestic production whatsoever, but some are predicting (hoping? wishing?) that one result of the Covid-19 global shut-down will be that at least some manufacturing moves back to American soil.

Let's take a look at some other aspects of the economy and what we can learn from other countries.

Government Pension Plans

Speaking of Social Security, let's talk about government pension plans as an alternative idea. These types of retirement plans are similar to Social Security, but you have the flexibility to choose how it's invested. You would be required to contribute, but you would also have a say in how that money is invested, unlike today's Social Security model where you're totally blind as to what's going on with your money. (And yes, it is your money - just like the money many of us squirrel away into IRAs and 401(k)s.) Remember, people who haven't saved - or worked - end up taxing our system anyway, one way or another.

The Australian Center for Financial Studies annually releases the Melbourne Mercer Global Pension Index which examines the pension systems of 20 countries across the Americas, Europe and Asia Pacific. The top 3 countries with the highest-rated government pension plans were Denmark, the Netherlands, and Australia. The United States ranked 14th. [80]

Let's look at the top three countries:

Denmark

Denmark received the highest score for 2015 of the 20 countries included in the index. As the world's leading pension provider, Denmark has a public basic pension scheme, a supplementary pension benefit tied to income, a fully funded defined-contribution plan, and mandatory occupational schemes. [80]

Netherlands

The Netherlands ranked number two, with an overall index value of 80.5 for 2015. Its retirement income system uses a flat-rate public pension and a semi-mandatory occupational pension linked to earnings and industrial agreements. Most of the Netherlands' employees are members of these occupational plans, which are industry-wide defined-benefit plans; earnings are based on lifetime average earnings. [80]

Australia

Australia ranked third in the Index, with an overall index value of 79.6. Its pension system is comprised of an income-tied, age-based pension funded by the government, a mandatory contribution from employers into a private fund and voluntary contributions into a private retirement fund. [80]

Poverty and Welfare

Per the 2018 US Census Bureau, approximately 38 million people live below the poverty line. That's about 11.8 percent of the population. Of the 38 million, almost 12 million are children under the age of 18. [81]

An estimated 59 million Americans receive welfare in an average month. That represents about 19 percent of the population. Of the 59 million, an estimated 2.25 million children receive welfare. [81]

Welfare-to-work

Per the 2018 Census Bureau, 109,631,000 people are taking federal welfare benefits. That equals 35.4 percent of all 309,467,000-people living in the United States at that time. [81]

I am not going to argue for or against the need for welfare programs such as food-stamps, unemployment insurance, Medicaid, WIC, Social Security, etc. That's for another book. What I will argue is that all recipients of welfare should do their part in returning to the system in one form or another. As it currently functions, there is no good incentive in place for anyone to try to get off of whatever welfare they're receiving, once they're on it.

Let's look to the state of Maine for an example of welfare reform that's working. The state passed a measure that requires recipients of the Supplemental Nutrition Assistance Program (SNAP) to complete a certain number of work, volunteer, or job-training hours before becoming eligible for assistance.

Then-Governor Paul LaPage passed the measure, and the resulting drop in food-stamp enrollees has been dramatic. At the close of 2014, approximately 16,000 individuals were enrolled in the state assistance program. Keep in mind that these are adults who aren't disabled, who don't have children at home, and who are claiming the food-stamp benefits because of a lack of financial resources. After forcing these individuals to either work part-time for twenty hours each week, enroll in a vocational program, or volunteer for a minimum of twenty-four hours per month, the numbers showed a significant drop from 16,000 enrollees to just over 2,500. [82]

Do you see what Maine did here? In a nutshell, they're making people exhaust their possibilities for employment before giving them a handout. Finally, a state government has hit upon a great way to reward people for trying to get jobs and to punish those who sit around feeding off the tax dollars of working Americans.

Of course, whether or not the rest of the country can work to adopt similarly effective laws is another thing entirely. But at least we have one example of how welfare-to-work type laws can be effective.

Departure Tax - Why Not?

On my first trip to Australia, I was surprised to learn upon arriving at the airport to head home, that I would be charged a departure tax before I could leave the country. At that time, it was roughly equivalent to thirty bucks. Obviously, this had no bearing on whether or not I would visit Australia. I did, however, wonder how Australia used that money, and why the US didn't charge something similar.

The revenue generated by this type of tax could be used to recover border control costs such as customs and immigration functions, to improve transportation infrastructure, to recover costs of maintaining common tourist attractions such as the Statue of Liberty and our national parks and monuments.

In my travels I've encountered this type of tax in several countries, including Austria, The Dominican Republic, Germany (factored into airfare), Mexico, and the UK. The average amount of the tax is $30.

If the United States decided to implement a similar departure tax of, say, a modest $20 per tourist (based on 2017 statistics), it would generate an annual income of more than **$1.538 billion** dollars. I can't figure out why we're not doing this.

Marijuana Legalization: Pros & Cons for the US Economy

Several states have already legalized marijuana in one way or another, and more dominoes are falling every day it seems. Since this chapter is about economics, the most obvious and important pro-legalization argument is of course a boost in revenue. Legalize it. Tax it. Get revenue.

But there's more. Legal weed could free up police officers and police funding to focus on violent crimes, rather than spending (wasting?) money on non-violent marijuana-related offenses. Federal prison space could also be freed up for more dangerous criminals.

The medical community could then spend more energy on utilizing marijuana for its beneficial purposes, including treating everything from PTSD to multiple sclerosis to Crohn's disease and of course, side effects from cancer-fighting chemotherapy.

Legalization of marijuana would also dry up revenue streams for the dealers, cartels, and terrorists who make enormous sums of money peddling illegal weed.

Of course there would be cons. Marijuana is an addictive substance that impairs judgment and can be abused, resulting in some very real health concerns. Second-hand smoke damage, reduced blood flow to the brain, lung, and heart heath and mental illness are all linked to marijuana use. Legalization could also increase accidents and make it more readily available to children. [83]

Whatever the pros and cons may be, it looks like more and more states are going to go the way of legalized marijuana. The government needs to make sure and take proper measures to capture the potential revenue stream as the illegal market dries up.

So, how much are we talking here? Some studies have indicated that around 20 million Americans have used marijuana in the last year, and that as many as 3 million (maybe - probably? - more) are daily users. And these are numbers collected after Nancy Reagan's omnipresent "Just Say No" campaign of the 1980s that aimed to reduce illegal drug use.

All the way back in 1994, Dale Gieringer, Ph.D., estimated in his piece <u>Economics of Cannabis Legalization</u> that, based on an excise tax of between fifty cents and one dollar per joint (or equivalent), the resulting revenue would fall somewhere between $2 and $7 billion annually. Add in a sales tax and you've got a significant revenue generator. In addition, hemp legalization could return this versatile crop to its previous levels as one of the country's top agricultural outputs. [83] Now, subtract what the country currently spends fighting illegal weed use and prosecuting and incarcerating users and dealers...well, you get the joint. I mean point. That's a lot of money, dude. [84]

The Best Countries For Raising Kids

If I asked you to name the best places in the world to raise children, what countries would you name? Top 5? Well, last year, US News ranked the best places to raise kids based on several attributes - human rights, family friendly, gender equality, happiness, income equality, safety, well-developed public education system, and well-developed health care system - and the top 5 are as follows:

Denmark, Sweden, Norway, Canada, and the Netherlands. Surely the US must be number 6, you're thinking? Nope. That's Finland. You have to drop all the way to the 18th ranking to find the US. We fall right between Portugal and Japan. [85]

I'm not going to delve in too deep here on what's wrong with this picture. This entire book is meant to point out how our government is failing us on all of these fronts. I'm just leaving you with a little food for thought before we move on.

The New "New Deal"

What exactly was the "New Deal"? On October 29, 1929, also known as "Black Tuesday", the stock market crashed, starting a chain of events that eventually led to the Great Depression. Let's take a deeper dive into what the chain of events was that caused the Depression by looking at an article written by Martin Kelly, The Top 5 Causes of the Great Depression:

The Great Depression lasted from 1929 to 1939 and was the worst economic depression in the history of the United States. Economists and historians point to the stock market crash of October 24, 1929, as the start of the downturn. But the truth is that many things caused the Great Depression, not just one single event.

...The stock market crash of October 29, 1929 was neither the sole cause of the Great Depression nor the first crash that month, but it's typically remembered as the most obvious marker of the Depression beginning. The market, which had reached record highs that very summer, had begun to decline in September.

On Thursday, October 24, the market plunged at the opening bell, causing a panic. Though investors managed to halt the slide, just five days later, on "Black Tuesday", the market crashed, losing 12% of its value and wiping out $14 billion of investments. By two months later, stockholders had lost more than $40 billion dollars. Even though the stock market regained some of its losses by the end of 1930, the economy was devastated.

The effects of the stock market crash rippled throughout the economy. Nearly 700 banks failed in waning months of 1929 and more than 3,000 collapsed in 1930. Federal deposit insurance was as-yet unheard of, so when the banks failed, people lost all their money. Some people panicked, causing bank runs as people desperately withdrew their money, which in turn forced more banks to close. By the end of the decade, more than 9,000 banks had failed. Surviving institutions, unsure of the economic situation and concerned for their own survival, became unwilling to lend money. This exacerbated the situation, leading to less and less spending.

With people's investments worthless, their savings diminished or depleted, and credit tight to nonexistent, spending by consumers and companies alike ground to a standstill. As a result, workers were laid off en masse. In a chain reaction, as people lost their jobs, they were unable to keep up with paying for items they had bought through installment plans; repossessions and evictions were commonplace. More and more unsold inventory began to accumulate. The unemployment rate rose above 25%, which meant even less spending to help alleviate the economic situation.

As the Great Depression tightened its grip on the nation, the government was forced to act. Vowing to protect US industry from overseas competitors, Congress passed the Tariff Act of 1930. The measure imposed near-record tax rates on a wide range of imported goods. A number of American trading partners retaliated by imposing tariffs on US-made goods. As a result, world trade fell by two-thirds between 1929 and 1934. By then, Franklin Roosevelt and a Democrat-controlled Congress passed new legislation allowing the president to negotiate significantly lower tariff rates with other nations.

The economic devastation of the Great Depression was made worse by environmental destruction. A years-long drought coupled with farming practices which did not use soil-preservation techniques created a vast region from southeast Colorado to the Texas panhandle that came to be called the Dust Bowl. Massive dust storms choked towns, killing crops and livestock, sickening people and causing untold millions in damage. Thousands fled the region as the economy collapsed. [86]

There are some eerily similar events today as to those that led to the Great Depression: 1) On March 9, 2020, the Dow dropped 2000 points, the largest single-day loss in the history of the stock exchange. 2) The US economy dropped at a 32.9 percent annual rate from April 2020 through June 2020, which is the worst drop on record. This officially puts the US in a recession. 3) Trump is in a Tariff war with China. 4) The unemployment rate sits at 14.7 percent, the highest since the Great Depression. What has stopped us, so far, from entering another great depression is the fact that the government has implemented multiple Coronavirus Aid, Relief, and Economic Security Acts (CARES) and that our bank accounts have federal backing preventing a "run on the banks".

So, what got us out of the depression? What was the government's response to that crisis? President Roosevelt implemented the New Deal, a series of programs enacted between 1933 and 1938. The New Deal focused on what historians call the three Rs: Relief, Recovery, and Reform. That is Relief for the unemployed and poor; Recovery of the economy to normal levels; and Reform of the financial system to prevent a repeat depression.

In the 1930s, there were major construction projects from coast to coast. The Hoover Dam, Triborough Bridge, Lincoln Tunnel, Empire State building, and La Guardia Airport are some examples. These infrastructure projects had a tremendous impact. They created jobs, jumpstarted spending and revived a sense of hope in the American people.

What we need today is another New Deal. We need to start investing in our infrastructure from coast-to-coast. We should be investing in things like Smart Cities, cellular, and IoT technologies. We should be incentivizing our young adults to seek out degrees in Architecture, Engineering, and Technology, focused on our future infrastructure needs. We can do this by reducing the cost of an education in these degrees.

I'm tired of hearing our Presidents talk about the need to improve infrastructure. I now want to see it actually happen.

CHAPTER 8 – ENVIRONMENTAL

"The Earth is what we all have in common."
-Wendell Berry - an environmental activist

As of 2020, the total global population is estimated at 8 billion people. That's a lot. It's more than double the global population in 1970, and The United Nations estimates that number will balloon to more than 11 billion by 2100. [87]

Folks, our planet is barely keeping up as it is. The rate at which humans - and especially Americans - consume the earth's resources is simply not sustainable, especially in light of these booming population increases and predictions.

Let's take a look at how much is left in the tank:

- Water – The Food and Agriculture Organization of the United Nations predicts that by 2025, 1.8 billion people will not have access to clean drinking water. [88]
- Coal – In 2011, it was estimated that we have enough coal to meet global demands for 188 years. [88]
- Oil – The BP Statistical Review of World Energy estimated that there were 188.8 million tons of oil left in the known reserves, and that was as of 2010. If current demand continues, this will supply the world demands for only the next 46.2 years. [88]
- Natural Gas – As of 2010, the known reserves of natural gas were estimated to last 58.6 years with the current global production. [88]

I found these numbers alarming, and if you didn't, you should probably read them again. Based on this data, by 2070, we will have depleted all of the earth's natural gas and oil reserves, and more than 2 billion people will be without drinking water. [88] That year was 2070. You and I may not still be around then, but our children will. It is your problem. And as Americans, it is definitely our problem. We comprise less than 5 percent of that 8 billion global population, and yet we use about a quarter of our shared fossil fuel resources: 25 percent of coal, 26 percent of oil, and 27 percent of natural gas. [89]

Drastic times require drastic measures, and we in the United States have not taken drastic measures to preserve these critical resources. It is our job - and our government's to lead - to find ways to reduce our consumption and stop taking so much more than our share. We should step up and set an example instead of turning a blind eye simply because we live in the land of plenty.

We're Wasting our Water

Now that I've painted the overall picture of this dire situation we've gotten ourselves into, I want to focus this chapter on water supply and conservation. As I'm sure you're aware, water is key to the survival of every living thing on the planet. An average human will survive about three weeks without food. Take away water? Only about three days. Water accounts for more than half of our body weight. Even mild or chronic dehydration can cause all sorts of health issues.

And yet, a frustrating truth about our great planet is that although its surface is more than 70 percent water, only about 1 percent of the earth's water is available to us. The remaining 99 percent is either saltwater or frozen ice caps.

Now, let's talk about the water we do have, and how much we're using. On a daily basis, Americans drink about 110 million gallons of water. An average family of four goes through about 400 gallons a day, most of that in the bathroom. Did you know that older toilets can use up to seven gallons per flush? Seven gallons! Newer toilets have cut that to less than two gallons per flush, but still. Are you one of the many Americans who leave the water on while you brush your teeth? You just wasted five gallons. In California, landscaping accounts for about half the water used in homes. Around 800,000 water wells are drilled each year in the United States for domestic farming and commercial use. [90]

Irrigation

The good news is that about 90 percent of the water we use in our homes makes its way back into the natural environment, replenishing water sources and eventually being reused for other purposes. One of the most wasteful uses of our precious water? Irrigation. Only about half ends up being reused. The rest either evaporates, is absorbed and released by plants, or leaks and is wasted. However, irrigation holds a longstanding place in our history, and is vitally important when it comes to food supply.

Irrigation is second only to drinking water in terms of its importance to humans. According to GlobalAgriculture.org, somewhere around 70 percent of the freshwater withdrawals on earth are used for irrigation. The global food supply would look very different if we didn't have water to nurture crops. And yet, the possibility of running out is real. Countries that produce high volumes of food such as China, Australia, and Spain, in addition to the US, are dangerously close to exhausting renewable water supplies. This is very bad news.

Not surprisingly, the areas of our country with both the highest irrigation water withdrawals and the largest amount of irrigated land are concentrated in states with low annual rainfall where crops are difficult to sustain. In fact, the states of California, Nebraska, Texas, Arkansas and Idaho alone make up half the total irrigated land in the country.

Where does this water come from? In the arid and mountainous western US, surface water provides the primary source of irrigation withdrawals. The midwestern states and Texas rely primarily on groundwater. Both are limited resources, and rivers, lakes and underground water sources are dangerously parched in many of these irrigation-heavy areas. And much of that precious water is wasted though leaky irrigation systems and inefficient application methods. Growing crops not suited to those arid environments also creates excessive amounts of wasted water. [92]

Widespread lack of awareness of just how bad this situation has gotten and the absence of effective environmental legislation only exacerbate the problem. We must do better. [93]

What Can We Learn from Other Countries?

Australia

Steps can and should be taken to mitigate this damage, and perhaps even start to reverse it, and the United States is behind. Australia is one country that has taken action. They have developed an extensive plan to use reclaimed effluent water for horticultural purposes. Simply put, wastewater is collected, treated, and put back to work for irrigation and other needs. Recycled water, in other words.

Australia is also taking action to reduce household water usage. Examples include requirements in Victoria that new house and apartment construction must meet the requirements of what's known as the 5 Star Standard. This means a 5-star energy efficiency rating for the building materials, water-efficient taps and fittings, plus either a rainwater tank for toilet flushing, or a solar hot water system. In South Australia, new homes will be required to have a rainwater tank plumbed into the house.

Sydney and New South Wales have established the Building and Sustainability Index, known as BASIX, which includes building regulations calling for a 40 percent reduction in water usage. A typical home can meet the BASIX requirements by installing showerheads, tap fittings and toilets with at least a 3A rating, and a rainwater tank or alternative water supply for outdoor water use, as well as indoor uses like toilet flushing and laundry.

In the Gold Coast, the construction of an 800-gallon rainwater tank plumbed into washing machines and outdoor faucets is mandatory in the Pimpama Coomera Master Plan area. Queensland offers a rebate of up to $1,500 for the installation of home rainwater storage. [94]

Germany

The folks in Germany have gotten creative as well. A so-called rain tax is collected based on a property's amount of impervious cover diverting runoff into storm sewers. The more rainwater is collected and conserved, the less water runs off. This in turn allows for smaller sewers and lower construction and maintenance costs. Citizens can earn rain tax reductions by converting impervious cover into porous surfaces. [94]

What Can We Do?

It's not all bad news here in the United States. Some states such as Arizona and New Mexico have established tax credits for conservation efforts and implemented rainwater collection requirements. In Texas, tax exemptions are available for water conservation efforts, and the cities of Austin and San Antonio offer subsidized rain barrels and rebates for cisterns to store rainwater. Even though our federal government is behind in its efforts, this is one area where individuals can make significant strides. [94]

Collect Rainwater

Let's talk a little more about cisterns and rainwater harvesting. Simply put, rainwater harvesting is the collection and storage of rain for later use to cut down on our consumption of and dependence on groundwater. Remember, a huge part of our planet is water. It's just unusable. Rain, on the other hand, can be collected and put to use for everything from drinking water to irrigation. The concept and execution are simple: underground cisterns collect rain siphoned from the roof and store it for later use.

Rainwater harvesting systems offer several advantages and are relatively easy to maintain. In addition to reducing the demand for groundwater, rain collection helps reduce floods and soil erosion as there's less runoff. For personal use, the roof on your home will likely serve as a good catchment area, and the water collected can be used to maintain your lawn, wash your car and clothes, flush your toilets and water houseplants. Using pure drinking water for anything other than hydrating the body is simply not necessary. It's an inefficient use of this precious resource.

Of course, there are a few disadvantages as well. Certain roof types don't work as well as others, and installing a cistern will come with an initial cost of anywhere from $200 to $2,000 depending on complexity. Like any home system, the cistern will need regular maintenance. However, those costs can be recouped in water bill savings over the life of the cistern.

To me, the advantages far outweigh the disadvantages, and it's my personal belief that the widespread and ubiquitous use of cisterns for rainwater harvesting is one of the best ways to start drastically decreasing our groundwater usage. Folks, this stuff literally falls out of the sky. Once your collection system is set up, you can simply sit back and wait for them to fill up. For free. And if you're not quite ready to install a full-fledged cistern, rain barrels that connect to your gutters and garden hoses cost less than a hundred bucks at Home Depot. It's not hard, and it's a start.

Install New Toilets

This is also a relatively simple and inexpensive way to reduce water consumption. Generally speaking, the older your toilet is, the less efficient it is. So, if you're looking for an excuse to start that bathroom remodel, buy a low-flow toilet and call it a water conservation project. Advances in toilet design and water efficiency have been made; you may have seen toilets that offer two flush options depending on, well, whether you're flushing a #1 or a #2.

The point is, there are steps we can take as individuals. But without requirements and incentives from our leaders, usage of these mitigating devices remains sporadic at best.

Desalination

Okay, I know I said all that ocean saltwater is unusable for human consumption. However, a process called desalination offers an option for putting this water to use. The city of San Diego recently spent a billion dollars (yes, that's billion with a B - I didn't say this was a cheap option) on a desalination plant. The facility takes ocean saltwater (plenty of that in San Diego!), removes the salt, and produces as many as 56 million gallons of drinking water per day. And that's nothing - a plant in the United Arab Emirates produces 564 million gallons per day.

Desalination is actually occurring more than you may think. As of 2013, 98 percent of the drinkable water in Dubai was desalinated. Saudi Arabia and Israel also utilize this method.

The drawbacks are big though - in addition to the cost to build, desalination plants guzzle a huge amount of energy and produce waste that could have negative environmental impacts. It's an interesting method to keep exploring though, and advances could always improve efficiency.

Wrapping Up

Of all of the earth's resources that we're wasting and in danger of depleting, water is perhaps the most precious. Without it, we die. We can't find an alternative for this one. Our government leaders must do a better job of advancing efforts to conserve water in both commercial and residential uses, and requiring citizens to do their part.

Charity – Sierra Club

"John Muir and a group of friends banded together in 1892 to ensure that California's mountains were protected and accessible to everyone. Since then, our scope has evolved to ensure that we're protecting the natural and human environment, but our purpose is unchanged: to bring people together to defend our natural resources and everyone's right to enjoy them."

Website - www.sierraclub.org/about-sierra-club

"With the new day comes new strength and new thoughts."
- Eleanor Roosevelt

When I started writing this book, back in the fall of 2015, I never expected to be writing a chapter on a pandemic. Actually, even after COVID-19 (severe acute respiratory syndrome coronavirus 2 (SARS-CoV-2)) was overtaking China, Italy, and France, in the early part of 2020, I was still not considering writing a chapter about a pandemic. However, I felt compelled to include this chapter when I witnessed how poorly our federal government handled the situation and how ill-prepared they were in stopping the massive spread throughout the United States. Let's face it, this isn't about whether you love or hate Trump, nor whether you are a Democrat or a Republican. This is about decisions (or lack thereof) that have caused many unnecessary deaths. This is about how the United States of America will probably end up with the worst statistics when it comes to the handling of COVID-19. You would think we were a third-world country. We had issues between State and Federal governments regarding who was responsible for securing ventilators, Personal Protective Equipment (PPE), and test kits.

Leading up to all this, the United States was expected to set an example for handling pandemics and actually help lead other nations by example. The following chart, from <u>The Global Health and Security Index</u>, lists preparedness for Pandemics by country. As you can see, the United States was ranked #1 [95]. This must now be an embarrassment since there are many countries that ranked much lower on the report that have handled the pandemic far better than the United States. Let's take a look at how we got where we are.

OVERALL SCORE		1. PREVENTION OF THE EMERGENCE OR RELEASE OF PATHOGENS		2. EARLY DETECTION & REPORTING FOR EPIDEMICS OF POTENTIAL INTERNATIONAL CONCERN		3. RAPID RESPONSE TO AND MITIGATION OF THE SPREAD OF AN EPIDEMIC	
Rank	Score	Rank	Score	Rank	Score	Rank	Score
1 United States	83.5	1 United States	83.1	1 United States	98.2	1 United Kingdom	91.9
2 United Kingdom	77.9	2 Sweden	81.1	2 Australia	97.3	2 United States	79.7
3 Netherlands	75.6	3 Thailand	75.7	2 Latvia	97.3	3 Switzerland	79.3
4 Australia	75.5	4 Netherlands	73.7	4 Canada	96.4	4 Netherlands	79.1
5 Canada	75.3	5 Denmark	72.9	5 South Korea	92.1	5 Thailand	78.6
6 Thailand	73.2	6 France	71.2	6 United Kingdom	87.3	6 South Korea	71.5
7 Sweden	72.1	7 Canada	70.0	7 Denmark	86.0	7 Finland	69.2
8 Denmark	70.4	8 Australia	68.9	7 Netherlands	86.0	8 Portugal	67.7
9 South Korea	70.2	9 Finland	68.5	7 Sweden	86.0	9 Brazil	67.1
10 Finland	68.7	10 United Kingdom	68.3	10 Germany	84.6	10 Australia	65.9
11 France	68.2	11 Norway	68.2	11 Spain	83.0	11 Singapore	64.6
12 Slovenia	67.2	12 Slovenia	67.0	12 Brazil	82.4	12 Slovenia	63.3
13 Switzerland	67.0	13 Germany	66.5	13 Lithuania	81.5	13 France	62.9
14 Germany	66.0	14 Ireland	63.9	13 South Africa	81.5	14 Sweden	62.8
15 Spain	65.9	15 Belgium	63.5	15 Thailand	81.0	15 Spain	61.9
16 Norway	64.6	16 Brazil	59.2	16 Italy	78.5	16 Malaysia	61.3
17 Latvia	62.9	17 Kazakhstan	58.8	17 Greece	78.4	17 Canada	60.7
18 Malaysia	62.2	18 Austria	57.4	18 Ireland	78.0	18 Chile	60.2
19 Belgium	61.0	19 South Korea	57.3	19 Estonia	77.6	19 Denmark	58.4
20 Portugal	60.3	20 Turkey	56.9	20 Mongolia	77.3	20 Norway	58.2
21 Japan	59.8	21 Armenia	56.7	21 France	75.3	21 New Zealand	58.1
22 Brazil	59.7	22 Hungary	56.4	22 Georgia	75.0	22 Madagascar	57.8
23 Ireland	59.0	23 Chile	56.2	23 Argentina	74.9	23 South Africa	57.7
24 Singapore	58.7	23 Singapore	56.2	24 Saudi Arabia	74.4	24 Micronesia	56.9
25 Argentina	58.6	25 Latvia	56.0	25 Albania	74.3	25 Uganda	56.5

Source: Nuclear Threat Initiative & Johns Hopkins Center for Health Security

The Horse was already out of the barn

I think we can all agree that there was no way to stop the spread of the coronavirus from entering the United States. However, it has been proven that the spread could have been slowed, lessening the number of American deaths as well as limiting the economic impacts. It has been proven by scientists that the coronavirus spread on the West Coast came from China and the spread on the East Coast came from Europe. Our Government was too slow in making decisions on stopping the influx of the virus. Also, due to reduced funding in the Centers for Disease Control

(CDC), our Government was not prepared for the multitude of decisions that needed to be made and the consequences of delaying these decisions.

Noah Higgins, William Feuer and Jasmine Kim published an article on CNBC on April 24, 2020, titled <u>New York Gov. Cuomo says the US acted too late to control the coronavirus: 'The horse had already left the barn'</u>

New York Gov. Andrew Cuomo said the US was too slow to respond to the coronavirus outbreak as it was proliferating in China in January, projecting that the virus had likely infected more than 10,000 New Yorkers in February.

"How can you expect that when you act two months after the outbreak in China the virus was only in China waiting for us to act? The horse had already left the barn by the time we moved," Cuomo said Friday at his daily press briefing in Albany.

Between the beginning of January to when the US closed its borders to Europe in March, approximately 13,000 flights from Europe landed in New York and New Jersey airports carrying more than 2.2 million people, Cuomo said. He said researchers now say the virus had likely infected 28,000 people in the US by that time, including more than 10,000 people in New York, in February.

The Trump administration declared a public health emergency on Jan. 31 and announced it would bar foreign nationals who have recently visited China from entering the US Although the virus originated in China, Cuomo said research indicates the outbreak in New York likely came from clusters of cases in Europe.

"We closed the front door with the China travel ban, which was right, even in retrospect it was right, but we left the back door wide open because the virus had left China by the time we did the China travel ban," Cuomo said.

New York, which has been the epicenter of the outbreak in the US, has more than 263,400 (as of May 23rd the number in NY State is over 358,000) confirmed cases of Covid-19 as of Friday afternoon, more than any country outside the US, according to data from Johns Hopkins University." [98]

Any way you cut it; this is going to be bad

He Could Have Seen What Was Coming: Behind Trump's Failure on the Virus Is an excellent piece written by Eric Lipton, David E. Sanger, Maggie Haberman, Michael D. Shear, Mark Mazzetti, and Julian E. Barnes for the NY Times and published on April 11, 2020. They go on to say:

An examination reveals the president was warned about the potential for a pandemic but that internal divisions, lack of planning and his faith in his own instincts led to a halting response.

"Any way you cut it, this is going to be bad," a senior medical adviser at the Department of Veterans Affairs, Dr. Carter Mecher, wrote on the night of Jan. 28, in an email to a group of public health experts scattered around the government and universities. "The projected size of the outbreak already seems hard to believe."

A week after the first coronavirus case had been identified in the United States, and six long weeks before President Trump finally took aggressive action to confront the danger the nation was facing — a pandemic that is now forecast to take tens of thousands of American lives — Dr. Mecher was urging the upper ranks of the nation's public health bureaucracy to wake up and prepare for the possibility of far more drastic action.

"You guys made fun of me screaming to close the schools," he wrote to the group, which called itself "Red Dawn," an inside joke based on the 1984 movie about a band of Americans trying to save the country after a foreign invasion. "Now I'm screaming, close the colleges and universities."

His was hardly a lone voice. Throughout January, as Mr. Trump repeatedly played down the seriousness of the virus and focused on other issues, an array of figures inside his government — from top White House advisers to experts deep in the cabinet departments and intelligence agencies — identified the threat, sounded alarms and made clear the need for aggressive action.

The president, though, was slow to absorb the scale of the risk and to act accordingly, focusing instead on controlling the message, protecting gains in the economy and batting away warnings from senior officials. It

*was a problem, he said, that had come out of nowhere and could not have
been foreseen.*

*Even after Mr. Trump took his first concrete action at the end of
January — limiting travel from China — public health often had to compete
with economic and political considerations in internal debates, slowing the
path toward belated decisions to seek more money from Congress, obtain
necessary supplies, address shortfalls in testing and ultimately move to keep
much of the nation at home.*

*Unfolding as it did in the wake of his impeachment by the House and
in the midst of his Senate trial, Mr. Trump's response was colored by his
suspicion of and disdain for what he viewed as the "Deep State" — the very
people in his government whose expertise and long experience might have
guided him more quickly toward steps that would slow the virus, and likely
save lives.*

*Decision-making was also complicated by a long-running dispute
inside the administration over how to deal with China. The virus at first took
a back seat to a desire not to upset Beijing during trade talks, but later the
impulse to score points against Beijing left the world's two leading powers
further divided as they confronted one of the first truly global threats of the
21st century.*

*The shortcomings of Mr. Trump's performance have played out with
remarkable transparency as part of his daily effort to dominate television
screens and the national conversation.*

*But dozens of interviews with current and former officials and a
review of emails and other records revealed many previously unreported
details and a fuller picture of the roots and extent of his halting response as
the deadly virus spread:*

- *The National Security Council office responsible for tracking
  pandemics received intelligence reports in early January predicting
  the spread of the virus to the United States, and within weeks was
  raising options like keeping Americans home from work and shutting
  down cities the size of Chicago. Mr. Trump would avoid such steps
  until March.*

- *Despite Mr. Trump's denial weeks later, he was told at the time
  about a Jan. 29 memo produced by his trade adviser, Peter Navarro,
  laying out in striking detail the potential risks of a coronavirus*

pandemic: as many as half a million deaths and trillions of dollars in economic losses.

- *The health and human services secretary, Alex M. Azar II, directly warned Mr. Trump of the possibility of a pandemic during a call on Jan. 30, the second warning he delivered to the president about the virus in two weeks. The president, who was on Air Force One while traveling for appearances in the Midwest, responded that Mr. Azar was being alarmist.*

- *Mr. Azar publicly announced in February that the government was establishing a "surveillance" system in five American cities to measure the spread of the virus and enable experts to project the next hot spots. It was delayed for weeks. The slow start of that plan, on top of the well-documented failures to develop the nation's testing capacity, left administration officials with almost no insight into how rapidly the virus was spreading. "We were flying the plane with no instruments," one official said.*

- *By the third week in February, the administration's top public health experts concluded they should recommend to Mr. Trump a new approach that would include warning the American people of the risks and urging steps like social distancing and staying home from work. But the White House focused instead on messaging and crucial additional weeks went by before their views were reluctantly accepted by the president — time when the virus spread largely unimpeded.*

When Mr. Trump finally agreed in mid-March to recommend social distancing across the country, effectively bringing much of the economy to a halt, he seemed shellshocked and deflated to some of his closest associates. One described him as 'subdued' and 'baffled' by how the crisis had played out. An economy that he had wagered his re-election on was suddenly in shambles.

He only regained his swagger, the associate said, from conducting his daily White House briefings, at which he often seeks to rewrite the history of the past several months. He declared at one point that he "felt it was a pandemic long before it was called a pandemic," and insisted at another that he had to be a "cheerleader for the country," as if that explained why he failed to prepare the public for what was coming.

Mr. Trump's allies and some administration officials say the criticism has been unfair. The Chinese government misled other governments, they say. And they insist that the president was either not getting proper information, or the people around him weren't conveying the urgency of the threat. In some cases, they argue, the specific officials he was hearing from had been discredited in his eyes, but once the right information got to him through other channels, he made the right calls.

"While the media and Democrats refused to seriously acknowledge this virus in January and February, President Trump took bold action to protect Americans and unleash the full power of the federal government to curb the spread of the virus, expand testing capacities and expedite vaccine development even when we had no true idea the level of transmission or asymptomatic spread," said Judd Deere, a White House spokesman.

There were key turning points along the way, opportunities for Mr. Trump to get ahead of the virus rather than just chase it. There were internal debates that presented him with stark choices, and moments when he could have chosen to ask deeper questions and learn more. How he handled them may shape his re-election campaign. They will certainly shape his legacy.
[99]

The CDC

The history of the Centers for Disease Control and Prevention (The CDC), as found on www.cdc.gov:

"On July 1, 1946 the Communicable Disease Center (CDC) opened its doors and occupied one floor of a small building in Atlanta. Its primary mission was simple yet highly challenging: prevent malaria from spreading across the nation. Armed with a budget of only $10 million and fewer than 400 employees, the agency's early challenges included obtaining enough trucks, sprayers, and shovels necessary to wage war on mosquitoes.

As the organization took root deep in the South, once known as the heart of the malaria zone, CDC Founder Dr. Joseph Mountin continued to advocate for public health issues and to push for CDC to extend its *responsibilities to other communicable diseases. He was a visionary public health leader with high hopes for this small and, at that time, relatively insignificant branch of the Public Health Service. In 1947, CDC made a token payment of $10 to Emory University for 15 acres of land on Clifton Road in Atlanta that now serves as CDC headquarters. The new institution expanded its focus to include all communicable diseases and to provide practical help to state health departments when requested.*

Although medical epidemiologists were scarce in those early years, disease surveillance became the cornerstone of CDC's mission of service to the states and over time changed the practice of public health. There have been many significant accomplishments since CDC's humble beginnings. The following highlights some of CDC's important achievements for improving public health worldwide.

Today, CDC is one of the major operating components of the Department of Health and Human Services and is recognized as the nation's premiere health promotion, prevention, and preparedness agency."

The CDC's current mission "CDC is a unique agency with a unique mission: We work 24/7 to protect the safety, health, and security of America from threats here and around the world.

CDC is the Nation's leading science-based, data-driven, service organization that protects the public's health. For more than 70 years, we've put science into action to help children stay healthy so they can grow and learn, to help families, businesses and communities fight disease and stay strong, and to protect the public's health.

*Our Strategic Framework and Priorities are **a bold promise to the Nation** (and the world). We will use our scientific expertise to bring a new level of preparedness in the US and global health security against current and growing threats, finally eliminate certain diseases, and bring an end to the devastation of epidemics."* [101[

In the following article <u>The CDC is a national treasure. Why is it being sidelined?</u> published on CNN by Jennifer Prah Ruger. She expresses her opinion regarding the CDC and COVID-19.

"Jennifer Prah Ruger is the Amartya Sen Professor of Health Equity, Economics and Policy and Founder and Director of the Health Equity and Policy Lab at the University of Pennsylvania. She is former member of the

US Centers for Disease Control and Prevention (CDC) Director's Advisory Ethics Subcommittee and former chair of the Ethics Special Primary Interest Group of the American Public Health Association.

Many years ago, I served on the CDC Director's Advisory Ethics Subcommittee. In the wake of SARS, anthrax attacks and avian influenza, the subcommittee's ethical guidance for public health emergency preparedness and response was important. Guidance stated that ethics should "inform advance planning and organization of emergency response so as to minimize the number of tragic choices that must be made."

Public health experts agree the US coronavirus response has been problematic. Rather than advance planning, we have repeated, and often conflicting, emergency responses. The number of tragic choices to be made is growing, not shrinking.

CDCs in South Korea and Taiwan helped those countries act swiftly, decisively and successfully against Covid-19. The Taiwan Centers for Disease Control activated the Central Epidemic Command Center and imposed home quarantines, border restrictions, a face mask distribution system and other preventative measures. The CDCs in Taiwan and South Korea spearheaded rigorous detection and contact tracing, communication, and isolation. Their coordinated approach explains their successes. The motivation: the memory of SARS and MERS. "We can't ever forget the incident. It is engraved in our mind," South Korean CDC's Lee Sang-won said about MERS.

The US, conversely, suffers from pandemic amnesia, a kind of collective myopia. Pandemic amnesia is a toxic combination of underestimated risks, insufficient preparedness and inadequate protection.

With SARS and MERS etched in memory, Taiwan and South Korea bolstered the capabilities of their respective CDC operations. The US, by contrast, cut CDC core emergency preparedness funding by over 30%, or $273 million from FY 2002 to FY 2017. Insufficient funding has meant public health labs have been understaffed or shut down, a keenly felt effect under Covid-19.

We've forgotten the CDC, a national treasure that successfully eliminated malaria in the United States and has worked heroically to control multitudes of infectious diseases known to humankind.

Pandemic amnesia is a malaise: a lack of focus, of conscientiousness and dedication, of motivation and stamina. These are risk factors for a different malaise, inept governance. Nothing in the history of humankind has killed more people than infectious disease. Still, initial momentum, investments and problem-solving -- and our memory of CDC successes -- quickly lapse as outbreaks fade and recede from view.

Pandemic amnesia threatens our health and security. Fortunately, we have a cure for that. Systemic reforms can save lives and money. The US needs to reinvest in the CDC to turn systemic fragility into resilience. Most importantly, we must acknowledge the CDC's critical role and we must correct misconceptions -- false beliefs -- that thwart pandemic preparedness.

The first misconception, the helplessness misconception, is that contagions are natural occurrences we can't control. This notion conflates naturally occurring viruses with human behaviors. Yes, a virus is natural. However, an epidemic is an increase in the incidence of a disease above the expected level. A pandemic is an epidemic's spread across multiple countries. While pathogens are natural, epidemics and pandemics occur through human behaviors that spread them. Weak policies, institutions and leadership foster these disasters. Pandemics are preventable and controllable. A strong CDC, as Taiwan and South Korea have shown, can and will play a vital role in controlling an outbreak.

A second misconception, the reactionary misconception, is the failure to focus on preparedness capabilities before disaster strikes. It ignores operational readiness. The belief that we can just deal with an infectious disease when it arises is false. The belief that risk is low and doesn't warrant warning people is false; risk awareness is indispensable. And the belief that the health care sector will save us is false. We need a strong public health sector and a strong CDC. Our current systems are inadequate. Focusing on prevention can strengthen these resources.

The prevention gaps are clear. We still lack a vaccine for HIV/AIDS, decades after its onset. Anti-vaccine sentiment is helping thwart US efforts to suppress even preventable diseases like measles, mumps and rubella.

"Vaccines are a victim of their own success," notes Dr. Paul Offit, co-inventor of the rotavirus vaccine. "We have largely eliminated the memory of many diseases."

Finally, a third misconception, let's call it the "it's the economy, stupid" misconception, is that pandemic preparedness is not an economic concern. As we've discovered only too painfully with Covid-19, this too is false. An unprecedented 33 million Americans have filed for unemployment insurance in the past two months; the jobless rate has almost quadrupled, to 14.7%. Covid-19's widespread health, economic, and social devastation will reverberate for years ahead.

Pandemic preparedness is significantly underfunded and underappreciated, given its health, social and economic benefits. But it is not visible to the naked eye. If we can't see it, it doesn't exist, and if it doesn't exist it's not in our memory.

The US faces a perilous choice: continued systemic fragility relying on repeated emergency responses with vast health, social and economic losses, or systemic resilience -- including a strong, fully-funded CDC -- to safeguard health and security. With the option to save countless lives at a fraction of the cost, the decision is a no-brainer, whether we suffer from amnesia or not." [102]

Impacts of slow response

So what are the repercussions of our Government's inability to adequately respond to the crisis in a timely manner?

James Glanz and Campbell Robertson provide the data on answering that exact question, in their article, <u>Lockdown Delays Cost at Least 36,000 Lives, Data Show</u>, published on May 20, 2020.

Even small differences in timing would have prevented the worst exponential growth, which by April had subsumed New York City, New Orleans and other major cities, researchers found.If the United States had begun imposing social distancing measures one week earlier than it did in March, about 36,000 fewer people would have died in the coronavirus outbreak, according to new estimates from Columbia University disease modelers.

And if the country had begun locking down cities and limiting social contact on March 1, two weeks earlier than most people started staying home, the vast majority of the nation's deaths — about 83 percent — would have been avoided, the researchers estimated.

Under that scenario, about 54,000 fewer people would have died by early May.

The enormous cost of waiting to take action reflects the unforgiving dynamics of the outbreak that swept through American cities in early March. Even small differences in timing would have prevented the worst exponential growth, which by April had subsumed New York City, New Orleans and other major cities, the researchers found.

"It's a big, big difference. That small moment in time, catching it in that growth phase, is incredibly critical in reducing the number of deaths," said Jeffrey Shaman, an epidemiologist at Columbia and the leader of the research team.

The findings are based on infectious disease modeling that gauges how reduced contact between people starting in mid-March slowed transmission of the virus. Dr. Shaman's team modeled what would have happened if those same changes had taken place one or two weeks earlier and estimated the spread of infections and deaths until May 3.

The results show that as states reopen, outbreaks can easily get out of control unless officials closely monitor infections and immediately clamp down on new flare-ups. And they show that each day that officials waited to impose restrictions in early March came at a great cost.

After Italy and South Korea had started aggressively responding to the virus, President Trump resisted canceling campaign rallies or telling people to stay home or avoid crowds. The risk of the virus to most Americans was very low, he said.

"Nothing is shut down, life & the economy go on," Mr. Trump tweeted on March 9, suggesting that the flu was worse than the coronavirus. "At this moment there are 546 confirmed cases of Coronavirus, with 22 deaths. Think about that!"

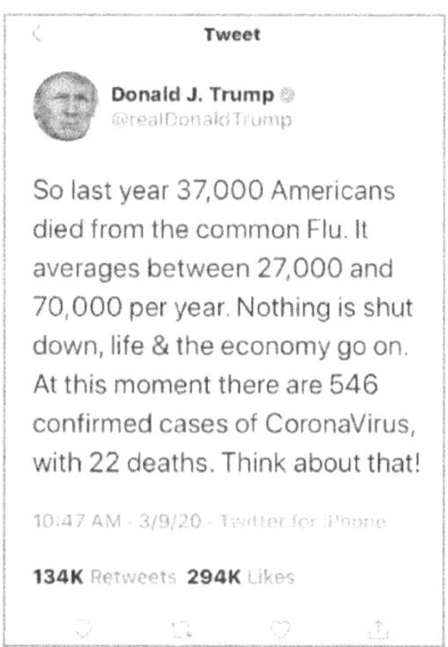

In fact, tens of thousands of people had already been infected by that point, researchers later estimated. But a lack of widespread testing allowed those infections to go undetected, hiding the urgency of an outbreak that most Americans still identified as a foreign threat. [103]

Update – June 30, 2020

Here are some staggering numbers as of June 30, 2020, according to Scottie Andrew of CNN.

The United States has long prided itself as the world's shining beacon. But its current status is a much darker one: the globe's leader in coronavirus cases.

More than 125,000 people have died from Covid-19 in the US, and more than 2.5 million Americans have been infected.

American life has been irrevocably altered by the worst pandemic in a century. And as the country struggles to reopen, cases of Covid-19 have surged again -- this time in young people and in states that had previously avoided the brunt of the virus.

The US death toll is more than twice as high as that of the country with the second-highest death rate, Brazil. That South American country has reported more than 57,600 deaths, according to Johns Hopkins University's global case count.

Leaders in both countries have continued to downplay the severity of coronavirus. President Donald Trump has refused to wear masks in public, which research has proven can control the spread of the virus, and has encouraged businesses to resume operations against the guidance of health officials who believe premature reopenings could lead to surges in cases like the US is seeing now.

Brazil's President Jair Bolsonaro called coronavirus a "little flu" and maintains that an economic shutdown would be worse for the country than the pandemic. He's also eschewed masks and social distancing guidance in public and has been criticized for underreporting coronavirus deaths. (Update: July 8, 2020: President Jair Bolsonaro has tested positive for Covid-19).

The US represents 4 percent of the world's population, but 25 percent of all coronavirus cases. More people are infected with and die from coronavirus in the US than anywhere else in the world. There are a few explanations for this disproportionate share of cases. The initial US response to coronavirus was slowed when the Centers for Disease Control and Prevention's coronavirus tests failed, delaying testing for weeks. And President Donald Trump throughout February downplayed the threat the virus posed to the US.

Health officials argue that February was a crucial time to contain the virus, and the US missed that window. Health and Human Services Secretary Alex Azar gave a similar warning last week when he told CNN's Jake Tapper that the "window is closing" for the US to get the pandemic under control.

Coronavirus has now killed nearly 126,000 people in the US since the first death was reported in February, according to Johns Hopkins University's case count. That's an average of around 1,039 deaths per day. The number shot up from the end of May, when an average of fewer than 900 people died every day in the US from Covid-19.

- *More than 58,000 Americans died in Vietnam. The US coronavirus death rate is 2.2 times higher.*
- *Almost 37,000 Americans died in Korea. The US coronavirus death rate is more than 3.4 times higher.*
- *4,431 Americans died in Iraq. The US coronavirus death rate is more than 28 times higher.*

- *2,445 Americans died in Afghanistan. The US coronavirus death rate is more than 51 times higher.*
- *More Americans also have died of coronavirus in less than five months than in all of World War I. That conflict took the lives of 116,516 American soldiers.*

The US may have missed 90% of people infected with coronavirus, according to an assessment by Dr. Robert Redfield, director of the US Centers for Disease Control and Prevention. With more than 2.5 million official diagnoses in the US, Redfield's estimate could mean more than 25 million Americans have been infected.

The lag in reporting is due in part to limited testing during the first few weeks of the pandemic. Now, as more people are getting tested, it's become clear that a large percentage of those who tested positive did not have any symptoms or had only mild symptoms, Redfield said.

More than 47 million Americans have filed for unemployment Fewer people have filed for unemployment benefits in June as businesses reopened, but many millions of Americans are still out of work.

Since mid-March, 47.3 million workers have filed for first-time unemployment benefits.

The US economy had its worst quarter since the 2008 recession. America's first-quarter GDP, the most expansive measure of the US economy, fell at a 4.8% annualized rate, the US Bureau of Economic Analysis reported in May.

It was the first contraction of the US economy since the first quarter of 2014, and the worst drop since the fourth quarter of 2008, the height of the financial crisis.

... and the worst isn't over. A staggering 36 US states reported a rise in cases last week. In Florida, officials recorded 9,585 new cases on Saturday -- a single-day record since the start of the pandemic. Just as states were beginning to reopen after lockdown, at least a dozen have halted their plans to further ease restrictions. [104]

Update – July 19, 2020

In an update By Remy Tumin and Elijah Walker, <u>Coronavirus cases are rising in 40 states across the country</u>:

More than 3,722,200 people in the US have been infected with the coronavirus, and at least 139,955 have died, according to a Times database. The country, logging a seven-day average of 65,790 new cases a day, has more confirmed cases per capita than any other major industrial nation.

Meanwhile, the White House is pushing to eliminate billions of dollars for coronavirus testing and tracing from a relief proposal drafted by Senate Republicans.

How did it get this bad? A Times investigation found that President Trump's failure to contain the virus can be traced to mid-April, when the White House rushed to shift responsibility to the states.

Here are some takeaways from our reporters' extensive reconstruction:

- *Key elements of the administration's strategy were formulated by aides who for the most part had no public health experience and were taking cues from the president. They were increasingly dismissive of Dr. Anthony Fauci, the nation's top infectious disease expert.*
- *Dr. Deborah Birx, a highly regarded infectious diseases expert, became the chief evangelist in the West Wing for the idea that infections had peaked and the virus was fading quickly.*
- *The White House was slow to recognize it had been wrong. Even now there are internal divisions over how far to go in having officials publicly acknowledge the reality of the situation.* [106]

The pandemic is highlighting yet another area where our nation is polarized. You have the "pro-mask" vs. the "anti-mask". The "anti-maskers" feel that their freedom is being taken away. The "pro-maskers" want an end to the pandemic and see the only way to contain the virus is by wearing masks.

When a nation is facing troubled times, what is needed is a strong leader to rally the people and to bring the country together to fight a common cause. During the Great Depression and WWII, we had FDR and his "Fireside Chats". During the Civil War, we had Abraham Lincoln. After 9/11, George W. Bush (even though I wasn't a fan of his) stepped up and brought our nation together.

Our country is facing the worst global pandemic in Earth's history. We are a nation that is divided, and unfortunately, we are without a strong leader. It's now up to us, you and me, to turn things around.

Charity – Feeding America

"Millions of children and families living in America face hunger and food insecurity every day.

- Due to the effects of the coronavirus pandemic, more than 54 million people may experience food insecurity in 2020, including a potential 18 million children.

- According to the USDA's latest Household Food Insecurity in the United States report, more than 37 million people in the United States struggled with hunger in 2018.

- In 2018, 14.3 million American households were food insecure with limited or uncertain access to enough food.

- Households with children are more likely to experience food insecurity. In 2018, more than 11 million children live in food-insecure households.

- Every community in the country is home to families who struggle with food insecurity including rural and suburban communities.

- Many households that experience food insecurity do not qualify for federal nutrition programs and need to rely on their local food banks and other hunger relief organizations for support."

Website - www.feedingamerica.org

"A house divided against itself cannot stand"
- Abraham Lincoln

As a country, we should be immensely proud of the many accomplishments we have made over the past 240-plus years. Admittedly, there are some very dark periods in our history as well but I believe when our Founding Fathers formed our government and established the Constitution, they had us, the people, in mind. They were breaking away from the Monarchy and tyrannical rule. They put checks and balances in place as part of our three branches of government. They aspired for a government that worked for the people. They viewed outside influences, like campaign contributions and lobbying, as corruption.

Our elected Government officials are no longer working for us, "the people". Instead, they are catering (or in some cases cowering) to those that have contributed to their campaign or contributed through the lobbying efforts of "big business".

The following was posted on Facebook on January 3rd, 2020 by Gregg Martin. The original article was written by Chris Sperry.

Twenty years ago, in Nashville, Tennessee, during the first week of January, 1996, more than 4,000 baseball coaches descended upon the Opryland Hotel for the 52nd annual ABCA's convention.

While I waited in line to register with the hotel staff, I heard other more veteran coaches rumbling about the lineup of speakers scheduled to present during the weekend. One name kept resurfacing, always with the same sentiment — "John Scolinos is here? Oh, man, worth every penny of my airfare."

Who is John Scolinos, I wondered. No matter; I was just happy to be there.

In 1996, Coach Scolinos was 78 years old and five years retired from a college coaching career that began in 1948. He shuffled to the stage to an impressive standing ovation, wearing dark polyester pants, a light blue shirt, and a string around his neck from which home plate hung — a full-sized, stark-white home plate.

Seriously, I wondered, who is this guy?

After speaking for twenty-five minutes, not once mentioning the prop hanging around his neck, Coach Scolinos appeared to notice the snickering among some of the coaches. Even those who knew Coach Scolinos had to wonder exactly where he was going with this, or if he had simply forgotten about home plate since he'd gotten on stage. Then, finally ...

"You're probably all wondering why I'm wearing home plate around my neck," he said, his voice growing irascible. I laughed along with the others, acknowledging the possibility. "I may be old, but I'm not crazy. The reason I stand before you today is to share with you baseball people what I've learned in my life, what I've learned about home plate in my 78 years."

Several hands went up when Scolinos asked how many Little League coaches were in the room. "Do you know how wide home plate is in Little League?"

After a pause, someone offered, "Seventeen inches?", more of a question than answer.

"That's right," he said. "How about in Babe Ruth's day? Any Babe Ruth coaches in the house?" Another long pause.

"Seventeen inches?" a guess from another reluctant coach.

"That's right," said Scolinos. "Now, how many high school coaches do we have in the room?" Hundreds of hands shot up, as the pattern began to appear. "How wide is home plate in high school baseball?"

"Seventeen inches," they said, sounding more confident.

"You're right!" Scolinos barked. "And you college coaches, how wide is home plate in college?"

"Seventeen inches!" we said, in unison.

"Any Minor League coaches here? How wide is home plate in pro ball?"............ "Seventeen inches!"

"RIGHT! And in the Major Leagues, how wide home plate is in the Major Leagues?

"Seventeen inches!"

"SEV-EN-TEEN INCHES!" he confirmed, his voice bellowing off the walls. "And what do they do with a Big League pitcher who can't throw the ball over seventeen inches?" Pause. "They send him to Pocatello !" he hollered, drawing raucous laughter. "What they don't do is this: they don't say, 'Ah, that's okay, Jimmy. If you can't hit a seventeen-inch target? We'll make it eighteen inches or nineteen inches. We'll make it twenty inches so you have a better chance of hitting it. If you can't hit that, let us know so we can make it wider still, say twenty-five inches.'"

Pause. "Coaches… what do we do when your best player shows up late to practice? or when our team rules forbid facial hair and a guy shows up unshaven? What if he gets caught drinking? Do we hold him accountable? Or do we change the rules to fit him? Do we widen home plate? "

The chuckles gradually faded as four thousand coaches grew quiet, the fog lifting as the old coach's message began to unfold. He turned the plate toward himself and, using a Sharpie, began to draw something. When he turned it toward the crowd, point up, a house was revealed, complete with a freshly drawn door and two windows. "This is the problem in our homes today. With our marriages, with the way we parent our kids. With our discipline.

We don't teach accountability to our kids, and there is no consequence for failing to meet standards. We just widen the plate!"

Pause. Then, to the point at the top of the house he added a small American flag. "This is the problem in our schools today. The quality of our education is going downhill fast and teachers have been stripped of the tools they need to be successful, and to educate and discipline our young people. We are allowing others to widen home plate! Where is that getting us?"

Silence. He replaced the flag with a Cross. "And this is the problem in the Church, where powerful people in positions of authority have taken advantage of young children, only to have such an atrocity swept under the rug for years. Our church leaders are widening home plate for themselves! And we allow it."

"And the same is true with our government. Our so-called representatives make rules for us that don't apply to themselves. They take bribes from lobbyists and foreign countries. They no longer serve us. And we

allow them to widen home plate! We see our country falling into a dark abyss while we just watch."

I was amazed. At a baseball convention where I expected to learn something about curveballs and bunting and how to run better practices, I had learned something far more valuable.

From an old man with home plate strung around his neck, I had learned something about life, about myself, about my own weaknesses and about my responsibilities as a leader. I had to hold myself and others accountable to that which I knew to be right, lest our families, our faith, and our society continue down an undesirable path.

"If I am lucky," Coach Scolinos concluded, "you will remember one thing from this old coach today. It is this: "If we fail to hold ourselves to a higher standard, a standard of what we know to be right; if we fail to hold our spouses and our children to the same standards, if we are unwilling or unable to provide a consequence when they do not meet the standard; and if our schools & churches & our government fail to hold themselves accountable to those they serve, there is but one thing to look forward to ..."

With that, he held home plate in front of his chest, turned it around, and revealed its dark black backside, "...We have dark days ahead!."

...And this my friends is what our country has become and what is wrong with it today, and now go out there and fix it!
"Don't widen the plate." [107]

The whole premise of this book is that our federal government is failing us. It is now up to us, as individuals, as "We the People" to stand up and demand change. Let's take examples of what other countries are doing and learn from them. Let's demand that the United States be competitive again in education, healthcare, and infrastructure. Let's lead by example with implementing new technologies, making conservation of natural resources a priority, and setting new gun control laws. Let's get back to valuing lives regardless of race, gender, religion, sexual preference, or political affiliation. It's time to hold our federal government accountable and insist that they not only step up to the plate but hit it out of the park.

Heart 911

"HEART 9/11 (Healing Emergency Aid Response Team 9/11) is a team of first responders - FDNY, NYPD, PAPD and the NYC Building Trades - that bonded in the aftermath of September 11, 2001 to honor the sacrifices of brave colleagues and family members lost, to continue to utilize their experience and training in service to others and to bring a message of hope to communities affected by disaster. HEART 9/11's mission is to Respond immediately to natural and man-made disasters; Rebuild community centers in hard-hit areas to meet grass roots needs; Recover by building resiliency for individuals, families and communities."

Built for Zero

"Built for Zero is a methodology, a movement, and proof of what is possible. The movement is made up of more than 80 cities and counties that have committed to measurably ending homelessness, one population at a time. Using data, these communities have changed how local homeless response systems work and the impact they can achieve.

Twelve of those communities have ended homelessness for a population by reaching a standard called Functional Zero. More than half of those cities and counties have achieved reductions in the number of people experiencing chronic and veteran homelessness.

Together, they are proving that moral courage, data-driven thinking, and a system-wide approach can build a future where homelessness is rare overall and brief when it occurs."

Jed Foundation

"JED is a nonprofit that protects emotional health and prevents suicide for our nation's teens and young adults. We're partnering with high schools and colleges to strengthen their mental health, substance misuse, and suicide prevention programs and systems. We're equipping teens and young adults with the skills and knowledge to help themselves and each other. We're encouraging community awareness, understanding and action for young adult mental health.."

Jack Kent Cooke Foundation

"The Jack Kent Cooke Foundation is dedicated to advancing the education of exceptionally promising students who have financial need. Since 2000, the Foundation has awarded over $200 million in scholarships to over 2,700 students from 8th grade through graduate school, along with comprehensive educational advising and other support services. The Foundation has also provided $110 million in grants to organizations that serve such students."

National Compassion Fund

*"The National Compassion Fund provides a single, trusted way for the public to donate **directly** to victims of a mass crime, such as a shooting or terrorist attack. It has been developed by the National Center for Victims of Crime in partnership with victims and family members from past mass casualty crimes, including those from Sandy Hook, Aurora, Virginia Tech, Oak Creek Temple, NIU, Columbine, and 9/11.*

The National Compassion Fund (The Fund) serves donors by honoring their intent and crime victims by distributing donations directly to them."

Sierra Club

"John Muir and a group of friends banded together in 1892 to ensure that California's mountains were protected and accessible to everyone. Since then, our scope has evolved to ensure that we're protecting the natural and human environment, but our purpose is unchanged: to bring people together to defend our natural resources and everyone's right to enjoy them."

Feeding America

"Millions of children and families living in America face hunger and food insecurity every day.

- Due to the effects of the coronavirus pandemic, more than 54 million people may experience food insecurity in 2020, including a potential 18 million children.

- According to the USDA's latest Household Food Insecurity in the United States report, more than 37 million people in the United States struggled with hunger in 2018.

- In 2018, 14.3 million American households were food insecure with limited or uncertain access to enough food.

- Households with children are more likely to experience food insecurity. In 2018, more than 11 million children live in food-insecure households.

- Every community in the country is home to families who struggle with food insecurity including rural and suburban communities.

- Many households that experience food insecurity do not qualify for federal nutrition programs and need to rely on their local food banks and other hunger relief organizations for support."

BIBLIOGRAPHY

Preamble – I Love My Country

[1] HBO TV show The Newsroom, A college student asks a panel "can you say why America is the greatest country in the world"? This was actor, Jeff Daniels', playing the role of Will McAvoy, response.

[2] Constitution for the United States of America.

Chapter 1 – Where it all began

[3] Tripnet.org - National Bridge News Release - 05/24/2013

[4] Gilded Age defined - Biographyonline

[5] Constitution for the United States of America, First Amendment

[6] History of lobbying in the United States – Wikipedia

[7] Harvard professor identifies the 'worst nightmare' in America right now Nicole Sinclair September 15, 2016 – yahooFinance

Chapter 2 – Foreign Affairs (a history lesson)

[8] The Untold History of the United States, By Oliver Stone, Peter Kuznick

[9] The Philippine–American War, Wikipedia

[10] Chile and the United States: Declassified Documents Relating to the Military Coup, By Peter Kornbluh, September 11, 1973, National Security Archive Electronic Briefing Book No. 8

[11] Kissinger approved Argentinian 'dirty war' Declassified US files expose 1970s backing for junta, Duncan Campbell, December 5, 2003

[12] The US-Iran conflict: A timeline of how we got here By Harmeet Kaur, Allen Kim and Ivory Sherman, CNN Published January 11, 2020

[13] United States support for Iraq during the Iran–Iraq War, Wikipedia

[14] Iran-Contra Affair, Wikipedia

[15] CIA Helped to Train and Support Bin Laden, Ramzi Yousef and Other Top Islamic Terrorists Who Bombed The World Trade Center, March 1, 2014, WashingtonsBlog

[16] How the CIA Helped Create Osama Bin Laden, By cganemccalla, Newsone

[17] US Secretly Gave Aid to Iraq Early in Its War Against Iran, By Seymour M. Hersh, January 26, 1992, NY Times

Chapter 3 – Infrastructure

[18] Global Competitiveness in the Rail and Transit Industry, By Michael Renner and Gary Gardner, September 2010, Worldwatch Institute, Northeaster University,

[19] Four things America can learn from Europe's trains, By Jon Worth, May 20, 2015, Politico

[20] How Politics and Bad Decisions Starved New York's Subways, By Brian M. Rosenthal, Emma G. Fitzsimmons and Michael LaForgia

Nov. 18, 2017, NY Times

[21] National Bridge News Release, May 24, 2013, Tripnet.org

[22] Where America's worst roads are — and how much they're costing us, By Christopher Ingraham, June 25, 2015, Washington Post

[23] The 11 countries with the best infrastructure around the world, by Elena Holodny, October. 2, 2015, Hong Kong Station, Wikimedia Commons

[24] Why Our Infrastructure Will Get Wet, by William Becker, August 17, 2017, Contributor Presidential Climate Action Project,

[25] Find Out the Differences between American vs German Homes: it's where the heart is, by Chad Josey, WORLDTHRUOUREYES

[26] Asphalt Roof Shingles vs. Slate Roof Tiles: Which One's Better? By Ben Matthews, August 30, 2017, BRAX Roofing

[27] Why we should bury the power lines, By David Frum, February 13, 2014, CNN

[28] www.everythingconnects.org/urban-sprawl

[29] smart city, Wikipedia –

[30] 5 Smart City Examples from Around the Globe, City Innovators by the Innovators Forum cityinnovatorsforum.com

[31] Singapore to spend US$1 billion in smart city initiative during 2019 By Asean Staff, February 11, 2019, CIO,

[32] The US Department of Transportation, Smart City Challenge

[33] How Four US Cities Plan to Fund Smart City Initiatives, by Mary Scott Nabers, June 22, 2018, IoT World Today

[34] Smart City New York: Cooperation to Innovation, HereMobility

Chapter 4 – Healthcare

[35] US Health Care Ranked Worst in the Developed World by Melissa Hellmann Jun 16, 2014 - Time

[36] The Commonwealth Fund, Mirror, Mirror on the Wall by Karen Davis, Kristof Stremikis, David Squires, and Cathy Schoen June 2014

[37] Life Expectancy Is Lower in Some Parts of US Than Iraq, the Philippines and North Korea May 8, 2017 – Newsweek

[39] universal-health-care-4156211, By Kimberly Amadeo, January 10, 2020 - thebalance.com

[40] Improving the prognosis of health care in the USA by Prof Alison P Galvani, PhD, Eric M Foster, Meagan C Fitzpatrick, PhD, February 15, 2020, The Lancet Medical Journal

[41] Fact Sheet: How much money could Medicare save by negotiating prescription drug prices? April 11, 2016, crfb.org

[42] <u>Big Pharma continues to top lobbying spending</u> By Karl Evers-Hillstrom October 25, 2019 - opensecrets.org

[43] Trump administration unveils executive orders to curb drug prices — but they come with caveats, by Nicholas Florko and Lev Facher, July 24, 2020, STATNews

[44] <u>Why is the infant mortality rate in the United States so high?</u> By Andy East, May 5, 2019, The Republic

[45] <u>8 Countries Doing Electronic Health Records Right</u> by Tera Rowland on April 3, 2012 – soliant.com

[46] National Alliance of mental Illness

[47] American Journal of Psychiatry and US Surgeons General Report 1999

[48] <u>Suicide rates among America's young people continue to soar,</u> by Jacqueline Howard, CNN June 18, 2019

[49] <u>Australia leads the world in personal control of electronic health records</u> by Hafizah Osman, December 12, 2018, Healthcare IT

Chapter 5 – Education

[50] The US was once a leader for healthcare and education — now it ranks 27th in the world, Business Insider

[51] thelearningcurve.pearson.com, index-comparison, 2014-lowest

[52] The US spends more on education than other countries. Why is it falling behind? by Dominic Rushe, September 7, 2018, The Guardian - Organization for Economic Cooperation and Development - Program for International Student Assessment - Program for International Student Assessment

[53] Cost of college countries around the world, Insider.com

[54] www.ny.gov, tuition free degree program excelsior scholarship

Chapter 6 – Gun Control

[55] Centers for Disease Control and Prevention, Web-based Injury Statistics Query and Reporting System (WISQARS), "Fatal Injury

Reports," last accessed Feb. 20, 2019, https://www.cdc.gov/injury/wisqars.Figures represent an average of the five years of most recently available data: 2013 to 2017.

[56] Centers for Disease Control and Prevention, Web-based Injury Statistics Query and Reporting System (WISQARS), "Nonfatal Injury Reports," last accessed Feb. 20, 2019, https://www.cdc.gov/injury/wisqars. The CDC warns that its estimates of nonfatal firearm injuries may be "unstable and potentially unreliable." To increase reliability of the data, a five-year average of the most recently available data (2013 to 2017) was used.

[57] Centers for Disease Control and Prevention, Web-based Injury Statistics Query and Reporting System (WISQARS), "Fatal Injury Reports," last accessed Feb. 20, 2019, https://www.cdc.gov/injury/wisqars.

[58] Centers for Disease Control and Prevention, Web-based Injury Statistics Query and Reporting System (WISQARS), "Fatal Injury Reports," last accessed Feb. 20, 2019, https://www.cdc.gov/injury/wisqars. Figures represent an average of the five years of most recently available data: 2013 to 2017.

[59] Mohsen Naghavi, et al., "Global Mortality from Firearms, 1990–2016," JAMA 320, no. 8 (2018): 792–814.

[60] Erin Grinshteyn and David Hemenway, "Violent Death Rates in the US Compared to Those of the Other High-Income Countries, 2015," Preventive Medicine 123, (2019): 20–26.

[61] Federal Bureau of Investigation, Uniform Crime Reporting Program: Supplementary Homicide Reports (SHR), 2012–16.

[62] Susan B. Sorenson and Rebecca A. Schut, "Nonfatal Gun Use in Intimate Partner Violence: A Systematic Review of the 54 - Literature," Trauma, Violence, & Abuse 19, no. 4 (2018): 431–442.

[63] JC Campbell, et al., "Risk Factors for Femicide in Abusive Relationships: Results from a Multisite [31] Case Control Study," American Journal of Public Health 93, no.7 (2003): 1089–1097.

[64] Federal Bureau of Investigation, Uniform Crime Reporting Program: Supplementary Homicide Reports (SHR), 2012–16.

[65] www.gunviolencearchive.org/past-tolls

[66] Wikipedia

[67] lawcenter.giffords.org/scorecard/

[68] Guns-and-Domestic-Violence, October 11, 2017, everytownresearch.org

[69] Background Check Reduce Gun Violence and Saves Lives, January 2017, Everytown for Gun Safety,

[70] Guns and Violence Against Women everytownresearch.org

[71] Canada bans assault-style weapons after its worst ever mass murder By Paula Newton, May 1, 2020, CNN

[72] How Have Your Members of Congress Voted on Gun Bills? By Danielle Kurtzleben, February 19, 2018, NPR

[73] When Lobbying was Illegal, by Alex Mayyasi, for Priceonomics.

[74] Alabama car dealership offers free shotgun, bible, and American flag to customers, by Hope Schreiber, June 25, 2019, Yahoo Lifestyle

[75] Gunman kills 2 at California car dealer, kills himself, by Nic Coury and Robert Jablon, June 26, 2019, Associated Press -

[76] Breaking down the NRA-backed theory that a good guy with a gun stops a bad guy with a gun, By Meghan Keneally, October 29, 2018, ABC News

Chapter 7 – Economics

[77] Why America is Going Broke, February 21, 2018, WSJ

[78] The Long Story of US Debt, From 1790 to 2011, in 1 Little Chart Matt Phillips November 13, 2012 – The Atlantic

[79] Why the US-China trade deficit is so huge: Here's all the stuff America imports, By Jeffry Bartash, June 25, 2019, Marketwatch

[80] Top Pension Systems in the World By Jean Folger March 16, 2016

[81] 2018 US Census Bureau

[82] New Report Proves Maine's Welfare Reforms Are Working Josh Archambault The Apothecary May 19, 2016

[83] Primary Pros and Cons of Legalizing Weed, NYLN

[84] Economics of Cannabis Legalization June 1994 by Dale Gieringer, Ph.D. Coordinator, California NORML

[85] Best Countries for Raising Kids, US News

[86] The Top 5 Causes of the Great Depression, Martin Kelly, Updated March 26, 2020, ThoughtCo

Chapter 8 – Environmental

[87] Wikipedia – World Population

[88] TheWorldCounts, November 7, 2014

[89] The State of Consumption Today worldwatch.org.

[90] Source epa.gov, watersense

[91] mojavewater.org and the American Water Works Association

[92] Estimated use of water in the United States in 2010, by Molly A. Maupin, Joan F. Kenny, Susan S. Hutson, John K. Lovelace, Nancy L. Barber, and Kristin S. Linsey – USGS

[93] GlobalAgriculture.org

[94] Rainwater-harvesting-inforesources, Water-harvesting-tax-credits, harvestingrainwater.com

Chapter 9 – COVID-19

[95] Global Health Security Index Report - Nuclear Threat Initiative, Johns Hopkins October 2019

[96] How the Pandemic Will End, by Ed Yong, March 25, 2020, The Atlantic

[97] Director of key federal vaccine agency says his departure was retaliation By Kaitlan Collins, Jeremy Diamond and Betsy Klein, CNN April 22, 2020

[98] New York Gov. Cuomo says the US acted too late to control the coronavirus: 'The horse had already left the barn', by Noah Higgins-Dunn, William Feuer, Jasmine Kim April 24, 2020, CNBC

[99] He Could Have Seen What Was Coming: Behind Trump's Failure on the Virus, By Eric Lipton, David E. Sanger, Maggie Haberman, Michael D. Shear, Mark Mazzetti and Julian E. Barnes April 11, 2020 - NY TIMES

[100] Hidden Outbreaks Spread Through US Cities Far Earlier Than Americans Knew, Estimates Say, by Benedict Carey and James Glanz April 23, 2020 - NY TIMES

[101] A Bold Promise to the Nation & Our History - Our Story, www.cdc.gov

[102] The CDC is a national treasure. Why is it being sidelined? By Jennifer Prah Ruger, May 15, 2020, CNN

[103] Lockdown Delays Cost at Least 36,000 Lives, Data Show, by James Glanz and Campbell Robertson May 20, 2020 - NY Times

[104] The US has 4% of the world's population but 25% of its coronavirus cases By Scottie Andrew, CNN June 30, 2020

[105] The latest predictions from Trump officials on unemployment numbers are dire, by Devan Cole and Betsy Klein May 11, 2020 – CNN

[106]. Coronavirus cases are rising in 40 states across the country, By Remy Tumin and Elijah Walker, July 19, 2020, NY Times.

Final Word

[107] 17 Inches by Chris Sperry posted by Gregg Martin January 3, 2020 – Facebook

ACKNOWLEDGMENTS

Writing a book, especially a non-fiction book, was much more challenging than I thought it would be. Since I am covering current events and every day there are news headlines that could be new fodder for the book, I wrestled with decisions like which topics to include and when to put the pen down. Thankfully, I didn't go this alone.

I'll start by thanking my awesome wife, Janet. She has been there from the beginning when this book was just an idea, and she encouraged me all along the way. Thank you for reading countless drafts, the never-ending edits and revisions, and for giving me advice on the cover design. This book is as much hers as it is mine.

Rebekah "Becky" Sellers, thank you for taking my research, thoughts, and ideas, and putting the pen to paper. You have been incredible to work with (and extremely patient). Thank you!

I want to thank Judy Poresky and Ken Zito, for agreeing at the last moment to read, critique, and edit my manuscript.

Joe Dintrone, thanks for the countless discussions and encouragement from the beginning.

Thanks to Vila Design for the ebook and print book covers. Tatiana was such a pleasure to work with

A very special thanks to Danny Prebutt for providing me with the inspiration to write this book. Danny proved that our 6th grade class from P.S. 49 in Queens, could produce (at least) two published authors.

And finally, I want to thank my kids, Caroline, Louis, and Rebecca. You have always been incredibly supportive and were great sparring partners when bouncing different ideas around. I also appreciate you being my biggest fans and going out and marketing on the various social media platforms.

ABOUT THE AUTHOR

John is a typical average American, who grew up in Middle Village Queens, New York. He attended college at the State University of New York College at Buffalo. He has worked in the Insurance industry for the past 32 years.

John lives in New Jersey with his wife and 3 kids.